The Organic Internet

Organizing History's Largest Social Movement

Alfredo López
Jamie McClelland
Eric Goldhagen
Daniel Kahn Gillmor
Amanda B. Hickman

Published by Entremundos Publications, 2007

Version 1.5

ISBN - 978-1-877850-00-4

Table of Contents

Preface

A note about language

Discussions of Information Communications Technology often refer to Free Software or Open Source Software. These terms are commonly used interchangeably, and indeed, their official published definitions differ very little from one another. For convenience, some writers merge the two terms and speak of FOSS or Free and Open Source Software, or use the term FLOSS to clarify that by "free" they mean "libre" (and not merely "gratis").

Because we, as progressive technologists, care deeply about the freedom of the people we support (including ourselves), we choose to use the term Free Software in this book. Free Software is about Freedom, not just visible source code or zero cost, and we believe freedom is an important goal. For a better understanding of why software freedom is important, please read the chapter by Amanda Hickman in this book. For more reading, and the official definitions of these specific terms, please visit http://fsf.org/ and http://opensource.org/

Stay Free!

Acknowledgments

This book was a collaborative project that involves more than the authors of the articles. Special thanks in particular to Mark Libkuman and Josue Guillen for reviewing the content, Jack Aponte, Nat Meysenburg and Jon Lorusso for copy-editing and everybody at the open staff meetings of May First/People Link for contributing to the shape of the book. The ideas in this book arise from countless discussions and ongoing activities involving the people who develop, shape, organize and are part of the Internet. They are, in essence, its authors.

Original cover art: Oscar Torres

Additional cover design: Ashley Kesling

The Organic Internet

by Alfredo López

Part I - The Human Connection

Introduction - An Exercise

Before you read on, try this.

Log on to the Internet.

Open a web browser and go to a page you've never visited before and click on the first link you see.

Read the page that opens and then click on the first link on that page. Do the same thing with the web page you're taken to.

Keep doing it for as long as you're interested.

It's probable that, within a click or two, you're reading words and looking at images from a person you don't know who could very well live in a place you've never seen.

If you do this exercise for an hour, you will probably visit websites from people in dozens of cities in this country and maybe several other countries.

In a few minutes you did something that, a decade ago, was humanly impossible and inconceivable for most of us. Using things now found in most American households - a computer, a phone line and some cables - you are able to communicate with an unprecedented number of people in ways that are deeper and more probing than ever before.

You can search the web for the next several years and not visit all the websites that exist. You can read innermost thoughts, reports on daily activities, ideas, shared information and life stories from more people than most of us would get to know in a lifetime. You can quickly develop a relationship with them that would take years to develop in the off-line world. You can see them through images on their websites and see the things they want to show you. You can write to them after a click on their email links. You can bookmark their site and actually make it your own regular destination.

You can experience similar interaction with libraries and schools and organizations and businesses and so much more than you come into contact with in your off-line life and, in a short time, this digital world becomes part of your real world. Tasks and activities you would normally do once in a while in real time turn into things you do with more frequency, more comprehensiveness and more effectiveness online.

In this world you've joined, many of the traditional separations between us disappear. Through the magic of hypertext links, any website can theoretically contain all other websites. You, as an individual, are related to all other individuals. Your activities as an individual are meshed with those of all others into a massive, uncontrolled and constantly-changing force that drives the Internet, defines it and changes it.

And all of that has changed your life in ways you probably seldom think about and may not even realize. The Internet is transparent, its influence on us stealthily seeping into the fabric of our lives - increasing its importance every time we log on and as we become more conversant and proficient in its use. We become reliant on it and defined by it without choosing to. We're caught up in this massive force quickly and without resistance.

Of course, this digital dimension is supported by something very real, concrete and even mundane. You're sending and receiving data through those phone lines or cables in small messages, called packets, from your computer to another computer that holds the information you seek, the sites you're looking for or the email account of the person you want to talk with.

That data uses a technology made up of complex sets of protocols which define how the computers must communicate and then transfer the data; infrastructure that directs the data you are sending or receiving to its target; and tools you use for email, web browsing and other Internet functions.

But you don't see any of that and probably seldom think about it. Instead, you're concentrating on the information you're getting and giving and the people who send it to you and receive it from you.

That is what's important to you and should be important to all who seek to understand and work with the Internet.

The Internet is the largest human network in history, comprised of an estimated 1.3 billion people worldwide who communicate with whoever they want, whenever they want, from wherever they are.

It changes fundamentally every second of every day as people log on and off and is growing in size daily. It has a culture and a history and a social structure. It's organic and only problems of a region's development or a government's interference limit it.

In fact, the Internet's technology has become so intertwined with the human experience that its very relationship to us has become organic; it has changed the role of technology in our lives.

It's uncontrolled, even out of control, and that's its real power. The traditional forms of control and repression used by governments and corporations have failed against the Internet, which either steamrolls over them or finds another way to deal with them. Of course, those forces are so intent on controlling the Internet that they're persistently developing more innovative ways to do it. And keeping the Internet out of their control is part of our movement's work.

To truly understand the Internet and to work effectively within it, we have to understand both the technology that drives it and the human network that uses it. That's not easy. In a society saturated with and stifled by alienation, our fetish with the props of our human drama too often clouds our ability to see and analyze what's really happening. We tend to see technology as physical things and this mistake makes it virtually impossible to understand technology and where it's going. Life has never been just the things we use and our future can never be envisioned based only on those things.

A telephone sitting idle on a desk isn't "mass telecommunications". An abandoned laboratory isn't "science". And wires and computers aren't the Internet. Exploring the Internet's implements in isolation will not, in the end, reveal much about the important questions:

Why has it grown so suddenly?

What role is it playing in our lives?

What is its future and its real potential?

For social activists and organizers these questions are critically important. The progressive movement has been a significant part of the Internet from its start and continues to play a vital role in its development. We use the Internet as a prime communications device in our organizing and our campaigns.

But is the act of using it enough? What if the Internet is more than a technology or even a network? What if it is a social movement in and of itself? If we progressives are in the midst of a movement of over one billion people, can we really be satisfied with our current role?

And what if that movement is crucial to the future of humanity? Can we reasonably interact with it without a strategy, coordination or organization? What will it take to develop that strategy? How do we strategically work inside a movement whose umbilical cord is tied to its technology? Must we rethink how we view movements and organizing if we are to succeed?

Put simply, what do we have to do to organize the Organic Internet?

Technology: the Constant Presence

Much is made of the Internet's newness, its speed and efficiency and the relentless addition of new tools, protocols and devices. The whole experience can be overwhelming and intimidating. It's scary, and the popular view of the Internet, fostered by our mass media, encourages us to fear it, to alienate ourselves from its real workings, to retreat to the safety of the user-friendliness that sits on its surface.

People often say, "I don't know how it works. I just follow the directions and...it works."

There's nothing wrong with that in practice. You should usually follow directions and it usually does work! In fact, the goal of technologists who work on the Internet is to make it easier for us to use and to make sure it works as often as possible.

But for activists, there is a danger in that ease of use. When we see something working and don't understand how it works, we tend to mystify it. That kind of mystification has given rise to a popularly held, distorted view of what the Internet really is.

People often tend to see the Internet as antithetical to normal human interaction - as if we were being turned into some army of controlled robots.

That frightening vision is beautifully illustrated in the *Matrix* movie trilogy. That these brilliantly-portrayed and thematically-rich movies have remained so popular hints at their visceral attraction. They reflect the uninformed and distorted belief that technology can acquire a mind of its own and ultimately control us, thrusting us into a false world, the delightful scenery of which masks an existential prison.

In truth, there's nothing unnatural or non-human about the Internet. It's only the latest example of humanity's relationship with our environment, reflecting the same human interactions and relationships we have always used to survive. Its roots are the very roots of human civilization.

One way of looking at the roots of the Internet is to imagine a group of people sitting around a fire a long time ago.

These people spoke a language that had fewer words than ours. Language is, after all, the way we communicate our needs to others, and these people's needs were limited to their environment - its potential and its dangers - and how they were relating to it.

One of those people was playing with a piece of wood (probably a broken branch), rubbing it against a rock and watching as the stick transformed itself, losing slivers of wood and becoming sharper. As the transformation took place, the others began to pay attention. Their eyes widened and their minds began to work. They were different from the other species around them because those minds were not only able to see what *was* there but to imagine what *could* be there; not only to *see* the sharpened stick but to imagine what it could *do.*

Another in the circle became agitated and began making downward motions with his or her hand, pointing excitedly at the ground. The stick holder stopped and looked at the thinker and soon the stick in his or her hand was thrust forcefully into the ground.

And it stood there, erect, as they all sat and watched in awe.

Over the next days or weeks or months, others began talking and thinking about the stick, about what else it could do. Some began experimenting with its integration into their daily routine of survival. These were geniuses, visionaries whose remarkable minds understood survival not only as the adaptation to the environment but as the alteration of that environment.

Over time the stick with the sharp point became a tool in that environmental alteration: hunting, gathering, cutting, building, securing, and defending.

And the rocks' edges could be sharpened to make knives or dulled to make striking tools. With these tools, and others they developed, their world could be transformed into an environment of nurture and nutrition. Its dangers could be shut out by structures and gateways. Its potential could be exploited and expanded.

They had technology.

There are, of course, many theories about all this and all are equally speculative. I have no idea if what I've described ever happened this way or if it was the first foray into technology. No one really knows.

But we can be sure that technology's roots lie in the deep ground of human cooperation and collaboration, driven by the need to survive and improve lives. We can be sure that the stick sharpener got the idea watching someone else do something similar. We can be sure that, if the group hadn't been sitting there or living with that sharpener or sharing their own experiences, imaginings and ideas with the sharpener, that stick would have been nothing more than a toy, a way to pass the time, an engrossing change one person experienced.

Technology is the collaborative act of humans using the environment to make tools to meet our needs.

As humans, our tendency is to collaborate; it's the way we survive. We have always done so and collaboration within our weak, small, slow and rather clumsy species has helped us to survive and, in fact, come to dominate the world.

Many other species cooperate; there are long lists of animals that form societies of all kinds, some of them pretty complex. But actual collaboration – the act of working together physically and intellectually, meshing ideas and configuring our ideas to incorporate the ideas of others – that's us.

We are collaboration's children and the Internet's technology is our collaboration's child.

Some people insist that the Internet isn't a function of human collaboration but rather an invention by a small group of scientists working with military support. In fact, the truth of the latter proves the former.

The Internet's technology developed during an Air Force-sponsored study and subsequent development program. But that's the technology and it's only the start. When you think about yourself, the assessment you make isn't based on what you were at the moment of conception or even the first months of your life; it's what you are now. What is important about the Internet isn't its initial life but its subsequent development.

It quickly became a kind of playground for technologists and more sophisticated users and their play attracted more and more people interested in nothing more than communication. In a historical blink of the eye, people all over the world were using it for email exchanges and information quests on the web and then developing their own presence on the web.

What's fascinating about the Internet's history is how, as more and more people began to use it, more and more began working on it collaboratively. And the drive of that collaboration over the next 20 years was always to massify it, to bring more and more people into it.

The question is: why? I think it's because the Internet is the most natural communications technology ever developed: the one that is closest to our most basic instincts and drives. It is inherently revolutionary and incompatible with any social and economic system developed up to now. Not only is it helping us develop our world, but it is actually transforming human and social behavior in a fundamental way.

The Metaphor of the Closet: the Struggle Against Alienation

To understand the nature, popularity and importance of the Internet, it's critical to look not at the tools we use online but at what we do when we're using them.

If we picture our lives in contemporary society as unfolding in a physical space, we might use the metaphor of a closet.

It's dark, restrictive and isolated. The door is closed and no information of any value can get in. We can occasionally, momentarily, and with some difficulty, push open that door a crack but we only catch momentary glimpses of others doing the same. There is so much we want to know about them but there's so little time before the door shuts again.

In this society, our psyches, social interactions, routines, and thinking are pushed into so many small, dark closets.

And yet we all keep pushing the door open. In a society that discourages truly deep and intimate human relations, we figure out all kinds of ways to counteract the painful alienation of the closed closet: personal relationships, organizations, events, and ways of sharing thoughts, feelings and aspirations. Yet, as rich and fruitful as we courageously make these things, they are never enough. We want and need to relate to more and more people in an ever deeper way, to grasp greater and broader realities, to learn more about everything so we can make sense of what we're experiencing.

The global communications infrastructure provided by the Internet is a function of that struggle, and its rise was inevitable. If we didn't have this particular technology, we would have used another. We are ready and our world begs for it.

Ravaged by misuse and destructive development, our world increasingly fails to function as an environment we can survive and thrive in. As a growing consensus of scientists now makes clear, our world is quickly becoming a hostile place. Huge masses of ice melt and threaten us with the destructive power of the water they unleash. The air we must breathe is so contaminated that it stifles us. The always precarious balance of nature between animals, vegetation and us is upended. It's no longer a subject of scientific disagreement: we are at the brink of catastrophic environmental collapse and the only disagreement is on how fast it's approaching.

The world economy is more than ever a model of discrepancy and imbalance, as a very small percentage of people get richer and the majority get poorer and poorer, the percentage of humans who are starving grows faster than ever, and the ravages of disease and malnutrition wipe out entire populations.

And we fight wars in numbers that have never been seen before. The people of every region in the world are now involved in some armed conflict which takes lives, consumes badly-needed resources and destroys living places.

We have no confidence that our children will live out a natural life. We fear that the world will be unlivable within our lifetime. We have no confidence that we, as individuals, can survive day to day. We are in crisis and we suffer the scathing insecurity that flows with that crisis.

What's more, the people who govern much of this world drive us apart. They seek to isolate us, to convince us that we're alone and that we're individuals whose well-being is pit against that of all others. We aren't producers; we're consumers. We aren't part of humanity; we are citizens of one nation or people of one race or members of one even smaller group.

Facing those challenges, we fall back on the one instinctive urge that has driven us forward: we kick down the door to reach out to others.

In fact, at its roots, every communications technology we've developed has been aimed at opening the door. In the end, all have proven limited.

We can phone only those we know and we can't see them when we do. We watch television, listen to radio and consume all mass media filtered through the perceptions, experiences and agendas of a relatively small group of people. We learn, for sure, we grow, possibly, but we seldom emerge more powerful from interactions with those technologies. The glimpses are longer and more comprehensive but they are still, in the end, only glimpses and the closet door always snaps shut.

The Internet's technology offers us, for the first time, a form of communication whose potential is boundless because, unlike any previous communications technology, it's not just a technology; it's a social movement that uses a technology. In fact, the technology has developed so quickly compared to previous technologies because it's being used by a social movement and that movement moves forward, naturally, through collaboration.

Faced with alienation, disunity and disempowerment that has brought us to the brink of personal despair, human annihilation and the physical destruction of our world, we respond as we always have, as our ancestors of so long ago did. We come together to collaborate.

The Organic Internet

It's a well-established truth that the development of the Internet's technology has been an act of collaboration; everything about this technology is the product of countless people - technologists, or techies - working together, driven by their desire to make it easier for people to communicate.

But what's different about the Internet is that the collaboration isn't only by those developing the technology; it's a collaboration among those using it.

We use its tools collaboratively, learning from each other and often being forced to learn new things by those with whom we want to communicate. You remember your first use of email? Why did you start? Probably because someone you wanted to communicate with needed you to.

That process of mutual learning is what actually creates the Internet's technology and expands it. To illustrate: techies are users themselves. Their inspiration for new ideas and approaches comes from their own use of the technology and their interaction with the rest of the Internet's users. In these groups, they collaborate on the construction of the Internet's tools and protocols, often working with people they have never met face to face, each contributing part of the code being written; submitting that code and changing it based on everyone else's suggestions and evaluations; intensely working together to issue beta (or testing) versions; and facilitating reviews and evaluations by test users all over the world which then form the basis of improvement and changes until the code is ready for final use by the Internet and is released.

It is a model of collaborative work, often without any financial compensation, driven by a belief in the Internet, a need for its technology, or a fascination with its power and capability.

The expansion of the Internet is also a product of collaboration by its users. The Web, the central star in the Internet's galaxy, has been constantly expanding, not because web developers come up with ideas on their own, but because people who use the web, work with it, develop its sites and visit those sites are constantly pushing to expand its use and letting developers know what's needed through a huge network of newsgroups, message boards and email lists.

Simple one-page sites and message boards give rise to blogs. Personal websites give rise to "Internet Personal Presences" like MySpace or Yahoo 360. People sending blind copies of email to lists of contacts often turn to email lists. Technological limitations, which always discouraged us from fully using technology, now become guidelines for expanding its use.

The Organic Internet

This is the interaction between a technology and people who are empowered by it, confident to use it fully, and make it more powerful when its capabilities fall short. Developers are simply skilled users who are listening and noticing.

The Internet's collaborative experience is markedly different from other technologies, not only in what it allows us to do but how much about ourselves it allows us to reveal.

With this remarkable combination of graphics, text, links, sound, and video, we can not only open the closet door farther but we can show more of ourselves when we do. We share not only snippets of our thinking or feeling or experience; we can now share as much of our lives as we want.

And in sharing our lives with others, we begin to alter the definition of truth. No longer is truth what someone with communications power says it is. With the Internet, millions of people can simultaneously express their version of truth, based on those lives and experiences they are sharing.

News is no longer only what reporters are saying; it's often what those making the news are sharing about their experiences. Analysis of events and issues is no longer just the few comments (from "both" sides) encased in the expressed opinions of the analyst or flashed on the television screen during a news show. Now we are exposed to hundreds, even thousands of "sides", often closer to the situation being reported on and usually more accurate. In the process, we collaborate on the truth, exchanging opinions and information and sifting through what we are exposed to with the filter of our own experience.

Never before in human history has such a process been possible, and that is the key to the Internet's impact. We are empowered to massively collaborate to identify what is true and then to unite to do something about it.

The Internet is the largest social movement in human history, and it is becoming a movement that comprises all of humanity. For progressive activists, the implications are huge.

The Internet as a Movement

About 25 years ago, in a late-night conversation with some organizers from the Mid-West, I was asked to describe my "organizer's fantasy". I was still drinking back then and the combination of beer and wee hours can nurture adventures in speculation.

I answered that I'd want a huge mass movement made up of people with diverse skills and backgrounds and I'd want to be an integral part of it - not just something I would join after it was developed or something I would "intervene" into or work to support. Not the usual organizer's scenario, but a movement spawned by a community of which I was an integral daily part.

I remember calling it an organizer's dream, and I think it is.

That's a situation overflowing with potential. And, for progressive activists, that's the Internet.

From the beginning, the American Left has embraced the Internet. Some of the very first websites were made by progressives and the progressive movement has been communicating via message boards and bulletin board systems, some of which actually predate the rise of the World Wide Web. When I founded People Link as a progressive Internet provider in 1995, there were already thousands of progressive Internet activities (sites and lists and message boards) going on.

It's pretty simple to understand the Left's interest in the Internet. Blocked from virtually every other avenue of mass communications, we found one that didn't and couldn't block us. Rather it allowed us to say everything we wanted to a staggering number of people. We seized it and learned to use it, and we have used it very effectively.

Maybe that success and unprecedented freedom of expression was so intense an experience for us that we couldn't take our eyes off it. Something certainly blinded us because, as the large network that was the Internet transformed into something much larger, very different and potentially of another strategic dimension, the Left in this country didn't seem to notice.

In fact, much of the Left continues to stubbornly hold on to the idea that this isn't a movement at all. And when one raises that possibility, some very committed, intelligent and Internet-savvy people either nod with glassy eyes or reject the idea outright. How in the world could anyone call the Internet a movement?

Well, the real question is how in the world could anyone consider it anything else.

Movements rotate around issues and the Internet is a movement around one of humanity's most pressing issues: alienation, one of the primary obstacles to all social change. Not only is alienation one of the central gears in the machine of our oppression - it makes successful unity more difficult and lack of unity breeds continued oppression - but it is, in and of itself, a painful, relentless and harrowing oppression. So the struggle against it is among our most important struggles.

Part of the problem is that, while we're busy struggling around so many issues, we don't realize we're struggling against alienation. It's so pervasive and discreet as an oppression that it's tough to notice it and our struggle against it.

But all attempts at effective communication, mutual support, shared constructive thinking, and decent, contributive relationships are effectively struggles against alienation. Our movement engages in these practices every day in our work and in the interaction with other activists. In fact, much of the human race engages in that struggle all the time.

This daily, heroic struggle – the relentless pushing against the closet door – is now massified and empowered by the Internet, and this movement's attributes reflect the breadth and scope of that struggle.

It is a genuinely democratic medium, usable by and accessible to everyone with access to a computer and phone line and to the Internet's technology itself.

It is world-wide and reflective of the world's unbalanced development. As of 2005, Internet usage was equally distributed between North American (U.S. and Canada), Europe and Asia with participation in Asian countries growing fastest and Africa and Latin America lagging way behind.

Its development has been an experience in the kind of mass, human collaboration just described.

It has developed its own culture: a language, a set of behavioral rules and, of course, a technology.

It absorbs other communications vehicles, including many of the most important modes of popular culture like television, movies, music and radio, each of which is now available in some form on the Internet. In addition to being an increasingly central part of people's daily lives, the Internet democratizes the production and distribution of popular culture, since anyone on it can now produce and distribute their own art.

It has returned the relationship of people and technology to one of popular empowerment by constructing a dialectic of influence in which its users change its technology constantly as that technology, and its use by so many people, change their lives.

Email has changed the way we speak with each other. The spider and web crawler protocols have transformed the way we get our information and learn. The World Wide Web has redefined how we present ourselves and see others. At the same time, each of these protocols change constantly with upgrades, improvements and alterations based on the expressed experience of the mass of people who use them.

This cycle of expressed need, tool development, impact on daily lives and tool refinement is as old as the human race. It is only very recently that much of the power over tool development has been largely removed from the hands of the mass of humanity. The Internet has reversed that alienating trend. The influence users have on tool design and development, the interactive and often intense way users and developers communicate about these tools, the fact that developers are actually users themselves and often begin developing these tools because they themselves need them - all these factors have never been present as deeply, routinely and massively with any other technology as they are with the Internet.

It has turned communication into an act of social resistance.

The alienation and separation fostered by our society continues to deepen due to the increasing atomization in our culture and the encouragement of the powerful. In ways that are both overt and subtle, we are discouraged from reaching out to each other on any but the most limited level.

The Internet is humanity's successful attempt to break through those barriers and, in this sense, participation in the Internet is an act of resistance against the powerful forces blocking profound, mass communication. Nothing else can explain the constant efforts the Internet makes to resist limitation and to find alternative ways of continuing and growing in the face of constant attempts to limit and misdirect it.

Even if someone found a way to shut down the Internet's current technology, the experience of communication so many people have had would result in the development of an alternative technology for the same purpose.

Independent of governments, corporations or other controlling powers, the people of the world are talking to each other in ways they haven't ever been able to before. That can't be stopped.

And finally, *it grows like a movement.* No matter what the commercial Internet does with its marketing, customer development and product releases, the Internet grows in one basic way: people who are experienced in it talk to others about it and help them become part of it. If asked about their own experience in getting on the Internet most people, I think, will remember somebody they knew and trusted telling them what to do.

As with any movement or campaign, the Internet's growth doesn't just happen; that growth is organized. It recruits. It sets up ways for new people to join it and encourages their participation. It arranges that participation and structures it.

Certainly understanding the Internet as a movement shouldn't discourage us from doing what we've always done with it: our "political work". But an understanding of its character as a movement alters how we define that political work. Not only does the Internet enhance our traditionally defined political work, but being part of the Internet is, in and of itself, political work.

The communication of progressive thinking on the Internet is no different than offering progressive ideas in a union meeting or a conference on the environment. Offering and developing technology can be as powerful as building a demonstration or organizing an action. In fact, the Internet expands the options we have for valuable issues and political work and it forces us to rearrange and re-prioritize.

We are today part of a larger movement around an issue that involves people of many political perspectives. We work in that movement, contributing to its struggles while logically injecting our own opinions and aspirations into its growing discourse.

When you log on, you are engaging in a political act: combating alienation through the mere act of communicating, enhancing the struggle against alienation by enhancing your use (and that of others) of the Internet's technology, and taking leadership by advancing your ideas about it - and the world.

So now we have a movement and we're a part of it. What do we do?

Part II - Organizing the Organic Internet

Introduction: The Activists' Hesitations

Many progressives are reluctant to view the Internet as a movement. That reluctance is most commonly expressed by two arguments that could be called "the activist's hesitations".

The first goes like this:

> Internet users don't view themselves as a movement, don't act in a coordinated fashion, are all over the place politically (including a very active neo-fascist segment) and, in fact, often engage in activities that are reactionary and socially harmful.
>
> How is that a movement and, even if we view it that way, why should we spend our precious time organizing it?

The moment we really examine this statement, it evaporates.

People who are part of movements frequently don't see themselves that way. It's not required. All that's required is that people participate in it for the reasons they deem appropriate. It's either a movement or not, regardless of what its members call it.

The idea that Internet users don't act in a coordinated fashion is patently absurd. The whole concept of the Internet involves coordinated activity.

Finally, movements aren't defined by the politics of their participants, but by the actions that unite them in this movement. In fact, it's often the case that progressive actions uniting a movement can have, in the short term, very non-progressive results.

No example better illustrates this than the U.S. labor movement. Clearly, not every labor movement member is progressive politically (and, by the way, many don't consider themselves part of any movement). The movement itself has often been embarrassingly reactionary on many issues. But progressives have always viewed that movement's unified activity - the struggle for better wages and working conditions - as the reason why the movement is worth our attention and effort. That struggle, we have always felt, is inherently progressive.

And that's true even when the conditions of our society or the strategies of the capitalist class end up making successes in that struggle harmful to others. For example, when capitalism meets our wage and conditions demands by cutting non-union workers' salaries and making their conditions more hellish, progressive unionists continue to fight for the wages and better conditions while fighting for union policies that protect those non-union workers as much as possible. In other words, they push for a progressive approach within the movement.

The struggle against alienation, the Internet's main thrust, is progressive even when a reactionary is engaging in it and in a society where relationships and psyches are distorted. It's not surprising that the Internet would harbor content that is sometimes pornographic, encouraging of a distorted self-image, or historically and culturally jaded. It reflects the people who make it up. Our job as activists is to work with those people, provide alternative visions and push for a progressive approach.

But that job is easier said than done because the character of the Internet changes things dramatically. This unique character gives rise to the second "hesitation":

> Internet work is fine, but it can't substitute for real "face to face" organizing.

What's interesting about the argument isn't its truth or falsity but that it is posed at all. In my experience, most of the people who express this hesitation don't use the Internet very much for their work or anything else. That's not a condemnation, merely an observation. But it's significant because for those who use the Internet, the supposed issue doesn't exist.

Very few activists who work with the Internet politically have abandoned face to face organization, and some say that their "real life" work has, in fact, been enhanced and broadened by their Internet work. Stands to reason: the more people you meet online, the more you're going to meet off-line. The Internet expands the available universe of personal contacts.

Not to say the concern is entirely made up. The Internet experience, if allowed to control our lives, can be isolating and addictively alienating. We are, after all, sitting in front of a computer communicating with people we can't see.

For activists, the problem is even more acute. The Left, with its constant stream of demonstrations and conferences, is not going to transform itself into a network of individuals who don't see each other - not very soon, anyway. It may appear that the two experiences are contradictory. They're not at all.

There is nothing innately alienating about the Internet. It's just communication. What's alienating is that you access the Internet in front of a computer, and a computer is physically too big to allow its entry into a large social space. In short, this "isolation" is less a function of the design of the Internet than it is the design of the computer.

Suppose the computer were small enough to carry in your pocket. Suppose all you had to do to log on was to push a button. Suppose your voice were all you needed to communicate digitally. No more keyboard, modem, or computer (as we know it).

What if every conversation between you and another, or a small group of others, could be turned into an international conversation, or if your discussions could be enriched by quick research without moving one step? What would demonstrations, conferences or other mass events be like?

What if, using the combination of Internet and video technology, we could actually be present during a war, or have a class of youngsters join another class on the other side of the world, or have a house meeting on some issue with households in several other countries?

Those scenarios and the potential they bring into relief are impossible to fathom. Our imagination about what's possible is limited by what is, and in our step-by-step speculation, it's difficult to imagine a world of digital/"real world" marriage.

Of course, the powers that be won't take us there. No corporate power is going to encourage the development of technology and protocols that allow for such open human communication. It would constitute an act of suicide on their part.

What's more, such advanced technology can be used to massify disinformation and confusion.

We, as a movement, have to develop the tools and protocols that can realize this potential, expand it and encourage its constructive use. We have to make it a reality because that, in the end, is our job.

Our hesitations are groundless. We have to take on the problem of organizing the Internet right now.

Different Types of Issues - Different Approaches to Organizing

In the progressive movement, we organize around issues. That's been the tradition in this country, and it's what's always worked for us. We define those issues by observing our lives and the places where pain and difficulty reside in those lives. Then we analyze what's wrong, why it's wrong, and what should be done about it. Then we help organize people to struggle for that cure.

The Internet doesn't change how we get our organizing cues from life, but it is changing life. That means that organizing the Organic Internet is going to require a major shift in the way we think about issues and organizing.

Lately there has been enormous discussion of some "Internet issues" involving access and freedom of expression. There has been some attempt to organize around these important issues. Some of us who understand the concerns are throwing ourselves into the effort and, in most cases, emerging frustrated.

Most of the Internet's users aren't interested in the issues we've been raising. This fact puzzles and confuses organizers. Why, given so much at stake, are so many people not getting it?

Maybe the problem isn't that they aren't getting it, but that *we* don't get it. Maybe the users of the Internet have defined other issues and are, in their own way, pursuing them. We progressives just don't see it happening.

Because the Internet is a technology-dependent movement, its primary issues are going to arise within the context of technology, and defining those issue areas is our first major challenge.

Here's how I would define some of them.

The Misdirection of Our Thinking and the Denial of Our Lives

Put another way, this is the struggle for access to free expression.

There are many countries on earth where people do, in fact, have legally guaranteed rights to freedom of expression. For most people, it's proven to be an empty tool; the stated purpose of that freedom, to allow us to influence others in our society, has been constantly frustrated. We can talk all we want, but our ability to actually reach people with our words and ideas is curtailed by the morass of cost, regulation and classist, racist and sexist filtering that makes it next to impossible to reach a massive audience with alternative thinking and information.

The Internet's technology changes all that; it is now possible to realize the social and political potential of freedom of expression.

Up to now, communications technologies have profoundly influenced popular ideology, as much analysis of television, movies, and radio consistently point out. But this influence is exerted primarily through the content communicated over these technologies. The shape of the technology doesn't change much.

The television is still a television and its fare is delivered in half hour or hour segments structured to allow for commercial advertising. It's been that way for its entire history, and the changes that have occurred (in cable TV, for example) are minor. The process is still the same: you sit down, you turn it on and it talks to you.

This same is true of radios and movies.

The Internet creates an entirely different relationship between us and technology. We have to be active. Unless we do something active, the content doesn't reach us. In fact, the real power of the Internet - that everyone can, for the first time in history, create his or her own content - expands that active role. And so the way we act and the tools we use to act become centrally important to the entire experience.

Those tools, and the technology of which they are part, influence the content of the Internet and direct how we are going to use it.

There's no better illustration of this than the MySpace phenomenon.

Using a simple, website-based formula combining already existing Internet protocols and tools, MySpace makes it easy for anyone to have a presence on the Internet and develop on-line networks of "friends," exchanging with them profiles of daily life, thoughts and feelings.

While this was always possible on the World Wide Web, MySpace made it easier for people to create a web presence for themselves without any knowledge of web design and management, and then tie that presence to others, exchanging media of virtually every variety. No real expertise was needed.

And suddenly young people, including large numbers of young people of color, were making their Internet presence felt. While that population had begun to grow in chat rooms (particularly on AOL) and among visitors to many websites, the act of creating web content had, up to then, been inaccessible to them.

In fact, this was an essential component of the "digital divide" argument made about the Internet, casting the problem as a kind of cyber-apartheid. But the problem wasn't color of skin or age or even class; the problem was access to a tool that young people could use to do what they wanted.

People want to meet other people and young people are no exception. They want to express themselves, exchange popular culture (like music and videos), they want to dabble in the all-too-taboo activities like sex. They want to communicate in a world in which they are respected and appreciated.

Constricted by their own isolation, pained by the need to reach out, challenged by the limitations of their geography and seething with a desire for intimacy and socializing, millions of people (a large percentage of whom are teenagers and young adults) have made MySpace the largest and fastest growing site in history. As of Sept. 8, 2005 106 million users had registered on MySpace and the system grows at an estimated 230,000 registrants a day. There is, at the time of this writing, no sign of slow-down.

MySpace temporarily satisfies those painful needs, but in the end, nothing changes. As is obvious from even a cursory review of MySpace blogs, those who use it continue to feel alienated, unsure of their future, oppressed by society's punishing pressures, and insecure about virtually every aspect of their young lives. While it allows a fuller expression of a life, MySpace doesn't change it.

And that's because, in the end, MySpace users are still alone. The tool itself, while encouraging communication between individuals, is structured to encourage individual expression, only serving to deepen the confusion and isolation. You can do a lot on MySpace, but the tools won't allow you to go beyond your individual life.

One of the obstacles to developing movements of human liberation is the persistent belief, drilled into us, that our lives aren't important or unique, that they lack any lessons others can benefit from. Effectively, our stories - rich in their portraits of human oppression and proof of the human ability to survive and move forward - remain untold, unshared, and unused.

We are taught that success in life is based on individual action and, battered by that ideology, we ignore the obvious: that it's through cooperation, reliance on others, building networks, and tapping our relationships that we survive, and it is only through that approach that we, as a human race, can progress. *That* story is vitally important for the rest of humanity to hear.

The way MySpace is built and designed makes such reflection and exploration virtually impossible. With an interface that is almost obsessive with the individual's life and an array of connections that relegate "friends" to an individual interaction, MySpace pages are completely devoid of any group or collective experience, and there is no obvious way to reflect such an experience.

This approach isn't driven by a conscious plan. Our society is saturated with the ideology of individualism, the best protection any capitalist society has. So we naturally tend to think that way. The problem isn't that someone is making tools based on individualism; it's that few are making tools to contradict or broaden that experience.

But it's vital for progressive people to view development of Internet technology as our challenge and not satisfy ourselves with using whatever tools are available at the moment. Someone is constructing those tools. Someone is guiding the Internet in particular directions. Someone realizes that the Internet's content is partly governed by the tools it uses. At this point, that someone isn't us, and it doesn't take much thinking to figure out who it is.

Either we take up the challenge or we lose the Internet.

The Access Issue

For the Social Justice movement, the primary Internet issue has always been access. Here the question is "access to what?"

For some time, social justice activists were fond of referring to "the digital divide": a term that described the lack of access to the technology that socially disenfranchised communities face. Activists variously approached that problem as either a reason to not rely on the Internet as a major organizing tool or to focus primarily on access as *the* issue.

In the developed countries, the issue quickly disappeared. The cure - getting people on the Internet - was easily delivered by capitalism as it sought to use the technology for marketing and to mold consciousness and culture. We didn't have to fight for it at all! While access remains a major issue for many parts of the world, the lesson we can learn from our experience is that this isn't the way to look at the problem of access.

Until the launching of MySpace, people of color and working people in this country were mainly consumers of Internet information. The attempts by communities of color to use the technology (e.g. *The Black World Today*) were, while earnest and rich in potential, controlled by groups of highly educated and highly skilled professionals. "Regular people" simply couldn't navigate the complicated and difficult tools necessary to do websites or even contribute to them.

That MySpace is the first vehicle that allows that kind of creative contribution is a reason for celebration but, as we just mentioned, it doesn't answer the Internet's real needs.

The critical issue of access isn't access to the technology, but access to power over how that technology is developed and used.

We are accustomed to viewing the development of technology as the work of highly-trained scientists, educated in specific disciplines, funded by large corporations, universities or foundations. They toil daily in a pristine lab setting, experimenting and testing until their product is ready for launch, and then it is introduced to the marketplace.

The Internet doesn't work that way. Internet techies arise from the Internet movement itself and never stop being users as they develop the technology. Effectively, they are the Internet's equivalent of grassroots leaders. As they develop the technology for the Internet, they exercise enormous power over the technology's function and, by extension, its content.

It is here that one of the Internet's greatest strengths feeds one of its major problems. For the most part, techies are white males, and since Internet technology is developed collaboratively by groups of technologists, the grouping follows social norms. In a society where racism and sexism are expressed in a kind of social segregation, non-whites, women and poor people are effectively often excluded from these groups. That the exclusion is mainly unconscious doesn't erase it.

The Internet is run by white men, and that demographic molds the content that is prevalent, dictates the way the tools used to produce that content are designed, and defines the needs that determine how those tools are developed. Until that changes, the problem of ideology mentioned above cannot be resolved.

Repression of the Internet

While the progressive movement hasn't completely understood the potential of the Internet as a social movement, other powerful forces in this country, particularly its corporations and many government agencies, have come to implicitly understand the potential threat it represents.

The Internet is organized and grows by its own form of organizing, but its true power is that it is uncontrolled and uncontrollable. That's the fulcrum of its democratic character. Historically, uncontrollable situations have sooner or later resulted in major social upheaval, and this isn't what governments and the capitalist class have in mind for the world.

As a result, the Internet is now an arena of an intense struggle between those who would control and narrow it and those who would set it free. This struggle saturates every advance and choice the Internet makes about its future, no matter how small that might be. Either the Internet gets more free or more repressive. There's no middle ground.

While this battle is fought in many areas, including the content and protocol issues we've mentioned above, one highly significant area is the exercise of policy and legal power over it. The past four or five years have seen the rise of policies, laws and procedures that are essentially repressive of the Internet and contradictory to everything it stands for.

The best known of these attacks is the intrusive blocking of email from users, usually using the pretext of blocking spam, or unwanted bulk email.

I'll defer to the essay on spam written by Jamie McClelland and appearing elsewhere in this book. He lays it out beautifully.

The same approach is evident in the laws around usage, the most recent of these being the attempts by some lawmakers, supported by certain large corporations, to limit Internet access through a system of special fees that would make certain websites more accessible than others.

The privacy issue reveals a particularly nefarious approach by the government to use the Internet for spying. In fact, most of us have no real privacy on the Internet and, if the government wants it, most commercial providers will immediately hand over all records and logs detailing who you are and what you've been doing on the Internet.

Finally, the quest for control is deceptively masked by the hysteria campaign around the Internet and abuse of children, pornography and child-stalking. This is an especially tough one for us. No one would argue that our society shouldn't protect its kids from predatory people and influences. These things are poisonous.

They are, however, lurking in every crevice of this society. They show themselves in virtually every aspect of popular culture. They are the dirty secret of American family life (a high percentage of child abuse occurs within the household). They plunge their poison into personal relationships of all kinds. They are there because our society is crippled by its vision of how people should relate to each other and how adults should relate to children.

Attempts to regulate the Internet to protect kids aren't pernicious in and of themselves. They can actually be productive. But those who seek to regulate Internet content with sweeping laws banning content aren't seeking to protect kids; they're trying to control the Internet.

Not one study has demonstrated that the Internet has expanded the abuse of kids in any way. While the advocates of Internet control scream about how dangerous it is, there is nothing to show that it is any more or less dangerous than streets, schools, or homes for that matter.

You can't be physically abused on the Internet, because the interaction isn't physical. Predators posing as children aren't harmful as long as they are on the Internet, because kids don't know they're adults. While it is certainly possible to abuse people through the Internet, the power imbalance and its resulting harm mainly happens when people attempt to expand their contacts into real life - something that actually seldom happens, and when it does it's an issue, not for lawmakers, but guardians, parents and friends.

No youngster should ever meet another youngster privately as a result of Internet contact. Period. That should be the rule for all households and it remains the primary guard against predatory abuse.

No Internet law can make that happen and none yet proposed would effectively combat predation or abuse of children. But most of those laws would constrict Internet expression so forcefully that many legitimate sites and content producers would be silenced.

The rule of thumb should always be that no law dictating Internet content should ever be passed or enforced.

And there are many lesser known issues lurking beneath the surface including how searching is done, how companies and providers can tag and trace you through the use of "cookies", how access to the Internet itself is handled and curtailed.

The relative lack of outrage about what is happening is probably best explained by the lack of consciousness on people's part about the Internet's character as a world movement and the importance it has to their lives. If progressives are still not clear about that, how can the rest of us be?

The Freedom of Technology

A debate has been raging within the Internet's technologist circles and it's remained hidden from most people, including progressive activists. It's over the use of proprietary software as opposed to free software. Free software is not about being free of charge: it is about being committed to software freedom. It is software that is free to be used in any way, free to be redistributed, free to be examined, and free to be modified, an integral part of the public commons. Free software is at the center of a critical issue for the Internet and the progressive movement.

Elsewhere in this book, Amanda Hickman writes superbly on several aspects of this issue. Her essay should be required reading for every progressive.

The bottom line is that free software is used in virtually every major activity on the Internet. Most common web servers and email servers are free software, as are many web browsers and email programs. Common software tools used to maintain and support the Internet are all built and distributed with freedom as an explicit goal. There are entire operating systems composed of nothing but free software. It just plain makes sense; there is almost nothing that a piece of proprietary software can do that some free tool can't do as well if not better. Free tools are, obviously, affordable to everyone, expandable by programmers when new needs arise and are frequently products of considerable testing and feedback from Internet users worldwide. They carry no onerous restrictions on their use.

What's more, they represent communities that form a centrally important part of the Internet. Viewed organically, a piece of software is a community. It is developed and upgraded by a community of developers and users. It is nurtured, critiqued, evaluated and popularized by a community through email, message boards and website comment systems. It grows with its community or, if that community evaporates, it disappears.

That's true of all software, free or proprietary. Communities formed around free software are unique in an important respect, however. While they are comprised of people of diverse political thinking, their members have in common an implicit belief in collaboration and mass participation - rather than profit and competition - as the driving force behind quality.

These communities not only foster software developed collaboratively, openly and with no restrictions on its distribution, but they have helped thrust free software into the central position in the Internet that it now enjoys.

Which raises an interesting question for the progressive movement: what if an alternative production system, developed collaboratively and nurtured democratically and freely, were to actually become the predominant system in an industry or section of the society or culture? How would the progressive movement evaluate that?

We would call it a victory - one that is virtually unprecedented in our movement's history. It would galvanize us, be a model for further struggles, become the subject of constant evaluation and lesson drawing for us.

Well, with free software, we've done that. We have won this struggle. And what's frustrating is that most activists in most of our movements don't realize it. That so many progressive people continue to use proprietary software, turning our backs on this remarkable victory, underscores this myopia.

But corporations do realize it, and victories can always be reversed. It's hardly surprising as the corporations move to control other aspects of Internet life, they are moving to virtually obliterate free and open source software, or FOSS.

Their tactics are a combination of the cannibalism and urge to hegemony that is stamped into the corporate genes and the use of laws and legal maneuvers that have always been among their primary weapons.

That hegemonic urge is on display in the monopoly strategy that characterizes the history of Microsoft and has been the subject of so much that has been written, said, and even litigated. It's brought into relief in the intrusive attempts by companies like Google to produce software (like its maps or spreadsheets) that are tied to its own corporate growth and would, effectively, capture and eventually limit the experience of Internet participants. It's highlighted by spasms of lawsuits, cases, threats, use of copyright and patent laws - the legal arsenal of corporations desperate to hang on to their market share and, they hope, increase it by eliminating or curtailing free software projects.

The challenge here is to protect free software, fight off any attempts to curtail it, use it, educate people about the importance of using it and participate in its impressive array of communities.

But that can only happen if the progressive movement realizes how important free software is and makes free software one of our priority issues.

The "Techie" as Leader

Among the most difficult Internet issues for the progressive movement is the role of the technologist.

Techies are the people who deal with the inner workings of networks, including the Internet. They work on and manage its file system architecture, its functions, its programs, the incredibly arcane system of ownership and permissions and all the things that pull all that together. They also deal with the physical nuts and bolts - routers, switches, connections, boxes (what normal people call computers). They are equally adept with a line of code and a screen of indecipherable status reports as they are with a screwdriver and a pair of pliers.

Clearly, these are not normal people. Most of us drive the Internet car, fully confident that it will start, stop, turn and idle pleasantly. Techies keep the motor working.

Hence the techie's plight. People rely on the Internet and expect it to function. In fact, we are often miffed when something doesn't work right. Most of us have no idea how close to a miracle it is that this fragile, incrementally developed system actually works. We tend to view a system problem as something that should never happen. When it does, we turn to the techie to fix it, often with impatience and sometimes with borderline hysteria.

And people seriously disrespect techies. They disrespect techies when seeking technical support in a screaming fit. They do it when a technologist graciously offers an explanation of a problem - how many people reading this have said "I don't care what's wrong, just fix it." And they disrespect techies when nothing is wrong and they can conveniently turn their attention to the Internet's explosive potential, completely forgetting about the men and women who make it possible.

If anything demonstrates this "invisible techie syndrome," it's what happened when the Internet industry collapsed a few years ago. Media stories abounded about investors' lost money, owners' lost dreams, communities' lost revenue sources, even people's lost email, but very little was written or said about the single greatest casualty: techies' lost jobs.

By some accounts, nearly 70 percent of all technologists in the Internet industry lost their jobs during that collapse as the workforce was cut down and many jobs shipped overseas to cheaper and more malleable labor markets.

Most of these people were left with no pensions, no severance packages, no health care, not even a months' notice. Their years of training and work were repaid only with the specter of shattered lives. And we lost a major weapon in the fight to protect and expand the Internet: the fact that an army of young workers in this country actually ran it.

We blew it, and we blew it out of a combination of ignorance, inflexibility and classist attitudes.

When the bottom fell out, most of the social justice movement was still blinking at the Internet in wonderment, like a child mesmerized by a toy display. We were trying to figure out how to use it, or if it was even useful at all. In the confusing mosaic, we couldn't see techies.

Perhaps there is a class attitude at work, because techies are the most physical and nuts and bolts of Internet people. They are our mechanics, our machinists, our repair people, and we all know how little respect these people get for the professionalism, skill, talent and commitment required to do their jobs. It's harder to pin down and harder to get people to admit to, but I think that classist attitude is part of the problem for our movements, including the labor movement.

All of which makes it difficult for us to accept the obvious: techies are today the leaders of one of the largest movements in the world.

This is probably the most difficult concept for progressive activists to understand. We have no problem understanding and identifying grassroots leadership. We can easily recognize a mass movement leader when we see one. We know, almost instinctively, who to speak with when we wish to work with or support a movement we recognize.

But this is different because this movement, which is technology-based, is completely unlike any we've dealt with before. The traditional leader's tools - public speaking, writing, face-to-face convincing, meeting and event organizing - are, while certainly present in many techies, not their most important leadership tools. Rather, their tools are the awesome expertise they have over technology.

Still, the basic criteria we use for leadership identification are all there.

What does a leader do?

Identify an issue or need, usually from his or her own life. Identify who else is affected by it. Start involving other people and getting them to involve other similarly affected people. And then have meetings, events and exchanges that discuss the issue and what to do about it.

That scenario, replayed in some form over and over throughout our history, is precisely how the Internet organizes and grows. It *is*, in fact, the history of the Internet.

Drawing on his or her experience as a user and countless communications with other users through email lists and message boards and simply providing support to users, the techie identifies some need. It could be a protocol improvement, an enhancement of a tool, a new way to approach infrastructure, or something less dramatic like a fix or upgrade or slight modification. No matter what, the techie's role is to define it.

The techie then figures out who's affected and will usually do this by posing questions or suggestions on one of the many email lists or message boards techies frequent. Collaboration immediately kicks in.

Creating that tool, the techie then beta tests it, involving a select group of people and quickly enhancing the collaboration. And those who are testing begin involving others - often by using the new creation to communicate with them. And then, when all that's done, they launch it and people use it to do something about the need that's been identified.

Yes, it is totally different from anything we've seen. But the criteria fit perfectly. Techies are organizers.

And so, here's the question: why does a movement whose organizations are often content and even elated by the participation of a few thousand people in a campaign or action around an issue not recognize the leadership of people who organize and lead 1.3 billion people?

Do we want to win or not? Isn't our goal to get people to work together? Because techies have figured out a way of getting a fifth of humanity to do just that. That is not something we can ignore.

Without the incorporation and participation of sizable numbers of technologists, progressives will not be able to organize the Internet.

Part III - A Strategy for Internet Organizing

With those primary issues identified, our movement's responsibility is to develop a strategy to progressively organize around them.

This work can't be done by one person or even a select group of people - the Internet itself must set this path - but our movement can work to focus Internet users in specific directions to help lead the focusing of the upcoming debate.

New Directions in Technology

For many of the reasons mentioned above, and many more, it is essential that the progressive movement begin an organized and coordinated effort to develop new protocols that guide the Internet in a more productive and progressive way. There are some protocols that seem particularly important:

- We need an alternative to the traditional email that has been around for over 20 years and whose weaknesses are exposed by the spam and security issues.
- We need an alternative "presence" tool or protocol that provides entire organizations and communities with the ability to project, act and interact with other such groups more efficiently than the web now permits.
- We need tools that join the personal or "local" digital experience (what you do on your own computer) with the Internet experience, thereby providing a more seamless relationship between personal and social experiences.
- We need protocols that, while using the domain name system, provide some independence from its constraints, providing us a method of self-identification that is consistent (away from the dynamic IP system), not tied to others (through a domain) and flexible enough for us to incorporate the powers of other protocols and tools (like audio/video communications).

The Access Issue

The curtailed access on the part of poor people, people of color and women to the technological leadership of the Internet effectively enslaves these people to the choices and judgments of groups of men, deepening the sexism and racism prominent in our society rather than working to combat it.

Since the Social Justice movement - where women and people of color play a central leadership role - has had stunning success in dealing with this issue, it's well positioned to work for these changes in the Internet.

There are many training programs for people but they all train people as users. What is needed is a huge, national training program - run by Internet techies - to specifically train people from the excluded groups to develop their real technological skills and a consciousness of themselves as organizers and with a commitment that these trainings will actually turn into working groups of technologists.

The Techie/Social Justice Movement Collaboration

The model for the treatment of techies by the Social Justice movement is atrocious and reflects our movement's inability to really see the Internet as it is.

Techies clearly have much valuable political and strategic thinking combined with the technological ability to put that thinking into organizing practice. In the appropriate atmosphere, their potential contribution to our movement is immense.

At the same time, it is important for our movement to understand the development of Internet technology - that mass collaborative experience - as organizing work.

Our goal should be two-fold:

- Techies should be involved as the organizers they are in all discussions and activities of all progressive organizations - not just technology-related activities.
- All projects to develop new Internet technology should involve non-techie progressive activists and organizers.

Software Should Be Free

No progressive organization should choose proprietary software over free software for anything. There's a stable, effective, free option for virtually every task you do on a computer, particularly on the Internet. If we can't find free software for a particular task, we should organize to develop it.

Additionally, we must resist any attempt by corporations to impinge on the free software movement, for any reason, including copyright or patent infringement. Using commercial laws to repress the development and use of free software is an obscene slap in the face of the Internet's culture and spirit and, in the end, damages its current functioning and its future.

Content Should Be Free

If we trust humanity to build a better world, we can trust humanity to make choices about what content is good and what's not worth the time, what's productive and what's damaging. We don't need our governments or authorities to make those choices for us.

All attempts to legally regulate content online should be viewed with great suspicion and, in most cases, met with sharp opposition. While there may be cases in which regulation might be acceptable, I have yet to see one identified.

To allow governments to regulate the Internet is to destroy its primary reason for being; that will quickly destroy the Internet movement itself.

Internet freedom is freedom of content.

Keep Power Over Email

You have a right to receive every single piece of email sent to you, and this is a right we must never give up. To give it up is to put the power over our communications in the hands of some company or small group of people.

The struggle over spam-blocking isn't a debate over how to handle spam; it's a debate over who has the right to make choices about an individual's communications.

We have plenty of spam identification software to help us flag spam. Even if you decide to automatically send all spam-flagged emails to the trash without looking at them, you are still exercising your right and power.

But once someone else determines that something they think is spam should never get to us, we've lost that critical power, and that's an invitation to censorship and repression. To not see that as a potential disaster is to stick your head in the sand.

A progressive demands that his or her provider deliver all email. If that demand isn't met, change providers and let them know why. There are more than a few providers who understand the dangers of spam-blocking.

(For an understanding of this complex issue, I again refer readers to Jamie McClelland's article on email.)

The Internet User's Bill of Rights

One idea worth considering in the face of attacks on the Internet is an Internet User's Bill of Rights. There are already several versions of such a document circulating on the Internet. I think a Bill of Rights that could be useful for organizing the Internet would summarize some of the issues I've mentioned above. For example:

- The right to receive every email sent to you
- The right to publish freely and on equal basis any website material
- The right to full access to the Internet
- The right to adequate and timely technical support

- The right to move and manage your own domain easily and transparently

This is certainly not a final version. It's just a few points I think progressives should be discussing for incorporation into a Bill of Rights.

Summing Up

For activists, there's no question the Internet is important. The real question is what's important about it.

We could continue as we are doing: using technology to reach out to people; to present information and our perspectives and to organize people around the issues we consider important.

Nobody would seriously argue that we should abandon using the Internet to organize around important issues. That would be foolish and a huge step backwards for progressive activists and movements.

That's why it's important to understand that the Internet is organic. Organic things aren't static; they move and change and progress. As the Internet evolves, somebody will lead and influence that evolution. Simply continuing with our present "just use the Internet" approach will ensure that the ruling classes, corporations and governments of the world will be able to define the evolution of the Internet to meet their needs and not those of the the majority of humanity.

They understand the Internet's organic nature and how important influencing and controlling it is. There is simply no way that those who oppose real social change, value profits over people, and see communications as a way of influencing and controlling people are going to accept a fifth of the human race communicating across every conceivable boundary. They have to control it and mold it.

They are doing that right now and we are the people conscious of that fact and able to take them on. Our experience has taught us how they operate and what they want and how to stop them.

That's the challenge, and there's an additional benefit in answering it. We are organizing the most important eruption of human resistance in history. As we work on its issues, it will naturally become more conscious of our issues - the ones we work on every day. They will see those connections because they are real. The struggle for an open, truthful and productive Internet is linked intrinsically to the struggle for freedom of expression and the just world that follows logically from it.

There's no blueprint for what to do. That will arise from the practical work and discussions people have all over the world. The only thing that's clear right now is that the work and those discussions have to start immediately and never stop until we all live in the kind of world we all deserve.

The Political Techie

by Jamie McClelland

During the late nineties and beginning of the 21st century, the landscape of people who provided technology support to nonprofit organizations in general, and progressive organizations in particular, changed dramatically. To take one marker: in the late nineties a relatively ragtag group of less than 100 technologists met annually under the banner of "Circuit Riders" to attempt to hash out a loose political vision of how technology can support the left. This gathering has since developed into the National Technology Enterprise Network conference drawing nearly 1,000 people and dozens of corporate vendors geared toward developing a professional association. This transformation has occurred, in no small part, as a result of a dramatic shift in funding. One of the major goals of the Circuit Riders - to convince foundations to support technology - has been so successful that the entire landscape has shifted.

This dramatic professionalization has had an enormous political impact on how we, as politically-minded technologists, operate. On the one hand, it has provided a basis for financial support. We are no longer forced to take organizing or other non-technology related job titles and then do both our "official" job and the job of technology worker. On the other hand, it has placed us in conflict with our role of providing leadership on technology issues.

The Conflict

Let's first consider what it means to be a political organizer using a classic example of a union organizer. For the sake of argument, let's ignore the state of unions in the U.S. today and instead focus on the methodology.

A union organizer typically will organize a non-union shop, where people are making very little money, have poor to zero job prospects, and in many cases are the sole earner for a family. The union organizer's job is to persuade them to organize, something that runs a very high risk of getting them fired. The organizer has to convince them to do something against their immediate self-interest, to take a major personal risk in order to get something much better in the long run, and not just for themselves, but for the entire group of people in the shop and the global labor movement.

The union organizer will often be criticized for not caring about the individual worker's well-being during the campaign. However, a good organizer, while caring about the individuals in the campaign, understands that the first priority is the bigger group; and that by taking care of the bigger group (i.e. unionizing the shop), the individuals in the group will be better cared for in the long run.

What does this have to do with technology? Well, if we were to use this analogy to examine the role most technology consultants provide to their clients, it would be closer to the union organizer picking off the wealthiest of the workers and individually counseling them on how to get a raise or a promotion. And, the consultant would be paid by that individual worker. After all, that is the model used by technology consultants when you consider the entire nonprofit sector. Rather than organizing the field of nonprofits for the purpose of using technology most effectively, technology consultants provide their services on a nonprofit by nonprofit basis.

I'm not making this analogy to say there is no place for technology consultants, particularly in the social justice world. Given the reality of technology and the social justice movement, we'd be lost without all the enormous work technology consultants provide to individual organizations. This work is vital.

The point of the analogy is to demonstrate the conflict between providing individual support to organizations and doing political organizing for the entire sector.

So how does this play out?

It often plays out when we are asked for a software recommendation. Let's take the office suite as an example.

As technologists, I think it's hard to argue with the idea that we would all be best served by having an open document standard. In other words, a standard way for saving word processor files, spread sheet files, etc that is controlled by a body that is (at the least) semi-independent of any single corporation and (at the least) semi-democratic.

With an open document standard, all the competing and various software programs that read and write office files could simply adopt one standard and voila: we have interoperability on a level we've never had in 25 years of office suites. Google, Microsoft Office, OpenOffice.org, KOffice, the gazillions of groupware programs, and future programs we've never even dreamed of could all read and write the same type of file with a reasonable expectation of having the file look and behave the same way.

So, how do we organize our people to make that happen? Again, if politics is our guiding principle, we organize a campaign with all the groups we work with to remove Microsoft Office (because it does not support an open document standard) from every computer within arms reach and install OpenOffice.org, which supports the best candidate for an open document standard (the "OpenDocument Format").

This strategy is not without some problems: it's going to cause organizations that have been dependent on Microsoft Office some pain - they're going to have to learn a new program, they're going to have to deal with poor translation of files between their partners who are still using Microsoft Office, and they're going to complain. Meanwhile, the technology consultant who made the recommendation is going to have to work harder, explaining why this is a good idea. And, the campaign to get all groups using OpenOffice might not succeed, which means the consultant will be taking a risk with an organization paying their bread and butter and may end up fired.

Yes. That's true and that's the conflict.

A good, seasoned technology consultant will respond to this issue with: of course there is a conflict. That's why the role of the consultant is not to make the decision for the client, but instead to layout the options and have the client make the decision. That's what client empowerment is all about. Too often consultants tell the client what to do and that's bad.

Agreed - telling a group what to do is bad. Forcing a group to remove Microsoft Office and install OpenOffice is not a good political or organizing move.

However, a union organizer does not walk into a non-union shop and say: "Here are the pros and cons of unionizing and here are the pro's and con's of working the way you're working now. I'm going back to my hotel. Give me a call when you've made a decision."

While a good organizer makes clear what the dangers and pitfalls are of building a union, the organizer is there with a mission and a goal and, most importantly, a bigger vision of a better world. A traditional technology consultant is there (by virtue of paycheck) only to help with that single organization's technology needs.

New Models

A big part of this conflict is how nonprofits pay for technology help. There is an entire industry which includes thousands of individuals, nonprofits and for-profits all with the goal of meeting the individual needs of each nonprofit and getting reimbursed by each individual nonprofit for the work accomplished.

In contrast, the group of people who got together in the late nineties referred to themselves as "Circuit Riders" because that name described a model of providing technology support: since at the time no single organization could afford to pay for a technology consultant, groups of organizations pooled their resources to pay one person who would serve all of their needs. While this was the hot topic of the nineties, the concept has largely disappeared in the United States (it is still being used abroad). It disappeared because groups became financially able to pay their own consultant to work for them and they realized that their individual needs were better met that way. And, of course, immediate individual needs are better met with an individual consultant working directly for you.

However, what about the movement? What about our long term needs? Given the dramatic swing of the pendulum from collective technology work to individual technology work, how can we continue to argue, debate, and hash out a vision for technology to support organizing? It may be time to go backwards and revive the Circuit Rider model, but not for individual consulting work, instead for doing the political work. The social justice movement needs individual technology attention, but it also needs a broader political vision and the political leadership in the technology world to support it and move it forward.

Domain Names

How the Internet Works Pt. I

by Alfredo López

In evaluating the issues facing the Internet and facing activists working within it, one thing becomes clear: our solutions are constrained by the technology's structure. There's a lot we can do within it but there is a lot we can't do.

What if that radical limitation - the structure of the technology itself - is the crux of the problem? What if our goal, in the end, is to not only organize the organic Internet but re-organize its technology?

To examine that problem, we have to have at least some working knowledge about how it now functions. This is the rub for many activists: technology is daunting and the mass media, with its tendency to mystify everything that occurs in life, hasn't made things easier. Most activists I know struggle to learn how to use the technology; the idea of understanding its workings is so overwhelming they won't even consider it.

But, as sophisticated as it is, the Internet is a simple technology. Its complexities reside, not in its basic functioning, but in capabilities and functions that are "added on" for security, efficiency or usability. They're the bells and whistles of the vehicle; the relatively simple motor hasn't changed all that much.

And, true to organic form, the Internet's technology starts and is based on people: its users. Like any massive congregation of people, the Internet's entire functioning is based on individual identity and everyone's ability to identify everyone else.

People don't realize it but, when you are in the Internet, you are clearly and distinctly identified.

The time you are logged into the Internet is called an Internet session and you start yours by communicating with your Internet provider. There are many companies and organizations that provide Internet access but most people use the larger ones like Earthlink, Comcast or AOL. They're people who charge you a few dollars a month, give you a telephone number to call through your modem (or a DSL line to hook up to your computer) and wait for you to log on.

When you log on, they have two roles to play:

They give you access to the Internet, making you part of the network - usually people call that "getting on-line".

And they stamp you with an identification number which is called an IP address or IP number. While there are variations to this (some DSL accounts have static IP address, for example), when most of us log on, our provider assigns us the next available IP address from a long list of numbers it has available. And this will change the next time with our next session.

To see what I mean, go to http://ip.mayfirst.org/. See that number? That's your current IP address - the id your provider has given you.

It all sounds nefarious, like some kind of national identification card that border guards can demand from you at gunpoint, but the IP address system is both necessary and extremely useful. We couldn't do the Internet without it and that becomes obvious once you're part of the Internet because, once logged in, nothing happens. Your provider has basically said: you're logged in, you have your id, you are now on your own.

It's like stepping into a huge room where a party is ongoing. You're there. Now what? If you don't do something, you will sit and stare at an inactive computer screen. So to begin communicating, you must exploit the Internet's vast and complex array of protocols and infrastructures.

Say, for instance, you open your web browser and enter the URL (or web address, like http://mayfirst.org/) of your favorite website. Since so much is now automated, it's probable that your browser already has a URL it opens automatically.

You have begun to use the Internet's best known protocol - hypertext transfer protocol (HTTP) - also known as the World Wide Web.

HTTP is a protocol for sending and receiving pages of text that are stored on computers (a lot like the one you use at home or office) in directories just like the ones you are familiar with (the "folders" you might find on your computer's desktop). The only difference between those text files and text pages you might write with a word processing program is that they include hypertext "links" - words that, when clicked in your browser send you to another text file on that computer or any other computer in the world.

In short, HTTP connects all the Internet's computers serving websites and seeking them.

To understand how this works, we have to keep in mind that stripped down of all its own bells and whistles, the web is mostly a bunch of text files on a bunch of computers. That's all it needs; that and your ability to find what you're looking for and be found by those looking for you.

That seemingly awesome task is handled by the Internet's traffic system which uses a protocol called DNS (Domain Name System).

This is a URL (or Uniform Resource Locator - a big term for "address"):

http://www.ussf2007.org/

You're used to it if you've used the Internet for even a day or two. It's ubiquitous on the web (and, in fact, in every other Internet protocol).

But it's full of vital information that tells your browser what to do and where to go.

The "http" is the protocol definition. It means "I'm looking for a hypertext transfer protocol" document on the Internet.

The "www" is a part of the website's host name that helps identify the particular website or document, but that comes into use later.

The most vital part of the URL is "ussf2007.org". That's the domain and domains are the fulcrum of the Internet's addressing system.

When your browser reads that URL it goes out to the Internet and starts making requests by talking to other computers - sending out small messages called data packets. In the data packet, it tells them your IP number (so they know who's talking) and it explains what you want (that website). It does this intelligently because if it started talking to every computer in the world things would slow down a lot. So the first place it goes is the provider who put you on line when you logged in. That provider's server, known as a "caching DNS server" will figure out the IP address of the URL you gave it.

And this is where it gets interesting.

The provider's "caching DNS server" first checks to see if anyone has asked about the website's host name recently. If so, it returns that same answer it sent before.

If not, then it must do some research to find the "authoritative DNS server" for the domain name - in other words, where is the server that is handling that domain and requests for websites and other Internet functions using it.

To find the "authoritative DNS server" it asks the "top level DNS server" who to ask. There is a top level DNS server for very domain ending. With a ".org" address, for example, the top level DNS servers are run by the technology affiliate of Public Interest Registry (PIR).

Top level DNS servers are huge computer systems, often housed at Universities or very large corporations, whose only function is to store domain names and the "authoritative DNS server" that can report what the

IP address of hosts under that domain are. Note: these computers do not know the IP address of the host name - they only can tell you which server does know the IP address. That's their job and they are registered and licensed by the Internet's governing authority to do that work.

In this case, for example, it reports that the "authoritative DNS server" for the ussf2007.org domain is either a.ns.mayfirst.org or b.ns.mayfirst.org (which are handled by May First People Link). Then, your provider's caching DNS server asks either a.ns.mayfirst.org or b.ns.mayfirst.org (if one is down, it asks the other) what the IP address of ussf2007.org and presto we've got an answer.

Your browser now knows where to send you to get the website you're looking for.

But what about registrars? You may be wondering how companies like Dotster or Go Daddy or Network Solutions fit in.

The answer is: They, and they alone, have the ability to update the top level domain servers. So, when you register ussf2007.org with Dotster, Dotster tells the PIR servers that your domain name is managed by a.ns.mayfirst.org and b.ns.mayfirst.org. After they do that, their job is over (until you want to change them).

That's why your website can be completely functional on your hosting provider's servers but nobody can reach it. Your domain registration may have expired. The important thing to understand is that this domain registration has *nothing* to do with your provider. You change providers, all you do is update your records with the new provider's name servers and your new site on that new provider's servers will soon be visible to the world.

Once your browser learns that the website is hosted with us, it comes to our servers and asks, through another data packet, "Do you have this website?" Now the full URL becomes important.

As providers, we have our own DNS system, replicated on a group of databases on our own local computers (or servers, as many people call them). Our computers now speak with yours. They quickly review our records and, if they find the site, they answer "Yes, we have that site. You can go to this computer and make your request" And we give it another IP address (the one identifying the computer that's holding the site).

Your browser then makes the final request and the computer that hosts your site will look through its records, identify where in its file system that site lives, and begin sending it to your browser. It will start with the site's "index" page (usually called index.html or index.php) and your website's design, with its links and structure, takes over the conversation with the browser.

Every new web page you ask for will be delivered using this process or a version of it. If the new page is in the same site, the process is quicker and more direct. If it's a page on the same server but another site, it's a bit more complicated. If it's another site on an entirely different server or provider, a version of the entire process is repeated.

The Internet Protocol

How the Internet Works Pt II

by Eric Goldhagen

IP, TCP, UDP, ICMP... The Internet Protocol is a subset of the alphabet soup of acronyms that most people interact with every day and never think twice about. Most of us think about TCP/IP as a heading in the Internet settings on our computers more than as the critical tool that makes the entire Internet run.

The Internet Protocol (IP) is a method that allows data to be sent from one computer to another. The collection of computers sending data using IP is known as the Internet. Each computer on the Internet has one or more numerical addresses. A computer's IP address identifies it among all the computers on the Internet.

Any data sent over the Internet using Internet protocols is broken up into smaller chunks of data. These chunks of data, called packets, contain a part of the initial data, the address they are being sent from and to, and an indicator of what part of the overall data is represented. These packets get sent from one computer to another until they arrive at the destination. This means that the packets that make up one message can be sent by different routes. They also can arrive in a different order than the order they were sent in. The Internet Protocol delivers them and the Transmission Control Protocol (TCP) breaks the initial data into packets and reassembles them in the right order on the other side.

To fully understand why IP is so critical to what we know as the Internet, it is important to understand some of the history of how the Internet developed.

Once upon a time, in a cold war long, long ago, people set out to create a method of passing data from one computer to another across long distances. In order for this communication to happen in a time of war, and because of the flaky nature of early computers, there needed to be more than one path between any two computers on the network. This way, one computer being down would not prevent other computers from communicating with each other.

This need established one of the two critical design elements that makes the Internet possible - a decentralized network.

Instead of having one switching station (much like your home local area network (LAN) where every computer plugs into one hub, switch or router and all communication passes through that one point) the network was designed to be decentralized. Where each computer on the Internet is a peer of the others and can act as start point, end point or intermediary hop.

While the discussions and planning for such a computer network goes back as far as the late 1950's, ARPANET, as the early Internet was known, sent its first computer to computer transmission on October 29, 1969. At this point, ARPANET consisted of 4 computers. (The first communication was the prompt LOGIN: from one host to another, which crashed one of the machines at the letter G, this incomplete communication was considered a radical leap forward in technology[1].)

The second critical design element of the Internet as we know it, is what's known as a "packet-switched" network, as apposed to a "circuit-switched" network.

While there were early experiments with packet switched networking, the initial version of ARPANET used a circuit-switching methodology.

Circuit-switching could easily guarantee error free transmission of long streams of data, but could not scale. In telecommunications, a circuit-switched network is one that establishes a dedicated circuit (or channel) between nodes and terminals before the users may communicate. Each circuit that is dedicated cannot be used by other callers until the circuit is released and a new connection is set up. Even if no actual communication is taking place in a dedicated circuit then, that channel still remains unavailable to other users[2].

In 1970, the same year as ARPANET started using NCP (Network Control Protocol, a circuit switched protocol), ALOHAnet, the first packet radio network, developed by Norman Abramson at the University of Hawaii, became operational. ALOHAnet then connected to the ARPANET in 1972[3].

NCP was designed to guarantee delivery of every data packet a user might transmit. However, as ARPANET grew larger and more complex, this made the network harder to maintain.

In 1974 Vint Cerf and Bob Kahn published a proposal called "A Protocol for Packet Network Interconnection" which specified in detail the design of a Transmission Control Protocol (TCP). Four years later, Jon Postel and others would promote a reorganization of the original TCP into two protocols:

---

1 Hobbes Internet Timeline, http://www.zakon.org/robert/internet/timeline/
2 http://en.wikipedia.org/w/index.php?title=Circuit_switching&oldid=98155310
3 Hobbes Internet Timeline, http://www.zakon.org/robert/internet/timeline/

- IP, to handle only addressing/passing along of packets of data, and
- TCP, which would actually worry about which packets had made it, which had to be resent and how to reassemble the data packets in the right order on the other end.

User Datagram Protocol (UDP) was added to allow applications that did not need the error correction and other processor intensive overhead of TCP access to the transmission abilities of IP directly (for streaming data, voice data, very brief communications like DNS, etc).

By breaking up data into packets and sending each of those packets through the best path at that moment, data can be delivered in a way that has been able to scale from the initial 4 computers on ARPANET to the expected 256 computer networks that IPv4 was designed around, to the massive worldwide network we all interact with on a daily basis.

Packet switching contrasts with circuit switching, by not requiring a dedicated connection between the two nodes for their exclusive use. The same path can be shared for packets that are part of many different communications between different hosts.

Packet switching makes better use of the bandwidth available in a network, minimizes the time it takes for data to pass across the network, and increases robustness of communication[4].

While TCP/IP is the basis of computers connecting to the Internet, there are other protocols that are used to allow all the routers on the Internet to know the routes to other machines on the net, such as BGP (border gateway protocol), methods that allow machines to have names that get translated behind the scenes to their IP addresses (known as DNS, a topic covered in a chapter by Alfredo López), and plans to modify IP (from the current IPv4 to IPv6) to allow for more numerical addresses, but other than recognizing their existence they are beyond the scope of this article.

TCP/IP created a unified suite of protocols that could be implemented on any OS or hardware platform, and as a result can be thought of as the enabling force of the Internet as we know it.

The reality of networking thousands if not millions of computers and the reality of trying to organize millions of people can inform each other.

In this case, I think it is critical to understand that what makes the Internet function is first a voluntarily agreed upon protocol that allows for individual differences in hardware and software as well as an established decentralized structure. Combined with the culture of transparency and

4 http://en.wikipedia.org/w/index.php?title=Packet_switching&oldid=103592679

community-centric models of open source development we not only have the Internet as we know it, but we also have some very interesting lessons to take with us in our political organizing work.

Technical Architecture Shapes Social Structure

An example from the real world

by Daniel Kahn Gillmor

When you use the Internet, most of your communications rely on many different computers co-operating with each other. The computers co-operate with each other because they have agreed beforehand on a protocol.

The protocols we use for communication shape not just the communications themselves, but social and economic structures beyond them. In the USA, we have seen how choices in infrastructure can shape social structure in the physical world. Our society builds highways, malls, and suburban developments while neglecting its rail lines, public spaces, and cities. In doing so, we discourage civic interaction while facilitating pollution and dangerously sedentary lifestyles. This article shows how choices in digital communications infrastructure can also have an effect on our social fabric by focusing on one small example out of many.

I'll discuss here a protocol in common use on the internet today: Transport Layer Security (TLS) and its precursor, the Secure Sockets Layer (SSL). These are used (among other places) in secure World Wide Web connections. TLS, as it is currently implemented, fosters the concentration of power and money among certain groups while hampering the public's ability to engage in trust-worthy, secure communications.

This is important because we still have an opportunity to choose the tools and protocols we use. By choosing our protocols, we can help move toward a social order we prefer. I'll present an existing modification to TLS which I think can move our online culture in a direction that is more democratically-engaged and less authoritarian.

TLS is only one small piece of the puzzle. There are thousands of protocols and tools in use on the Internet today, with a variety of subtle societal effects. We can choose the way we want to go, but we can choose well only if we understand the issues!

Background and introduction

This article has a relatively narrow technical focus, but it's one which most people reading probably encounter every week, when using the World Wide Web (www).

What is HTTPS and why do we use it?

Most of your everyday use of the www consists of HyperText Transfer Protocol (HTTP) connections. This is the http:// you see at the beginning of many web addresses (known as Uniform Resource Locators, or URLs). An HTTP session consists of your web browser sending a request to the remote web server, which is just another computer connected to the internet. Your request consists of several things, potentially including:

- the full URL of the page you are viewing,
- identifying information about your web browser,
- small pieces of data called cookies,
- the contents of any form fields you might have filled in.

The web server replies to your request with its own information, potentially including:

- information about the page you requested,
- identifying information about the web server itself,
- more cookies,
- the contents of the page requested.

These communications (in both directions) are all visible to any computer along the way between your computer and the web server. If you included some information that you'd rather keep private (for example, if you typed your bank account number in a field of a web form), you might be upset that the intermediate machines can all snoop! Even worse, if your password is included in this information, the snooper could then use that password to take actions that only you should be allowed to take, such as updating your organization's web page, transferring money, making travel reservations, etc.

So just using unencrypted, plain HTTP is dangerously insecure! If you are anonymously reporting unethical activity of your employer, you do not want your employer (who controls the network you are using) to see what you are doing, or to alter the contents of your complaint as it is in transit. If you are dealing with your bank, you don't want the other machines on the network to be able to get information about your accounts, much less to withdraw money from them. We need some sort of way to keep our communications private and secure.

This is exactly why we use HTTPS, the secure version of HTTP. This protocol can be identified by the fact that the URL in your browser's address bar begins with https://. It is also often indicated by the little lock icon in your browser.

HTTPS is the same protocol as HTTP, but wrapped inside a layer of strong encryption. The encryption provides your communication with two things: privacy and integrity. Privacy means that computers other than your own machine and the web server will see the communications as a stream of gobbledy-gook, but your web browser and the web server involved will be able to understand them. Integrity means that both parties can be certain that the information they receive is actually the same information that was sent by the other party.

secure.mayfirst.org

The lock in my browser

This is a good thing, but some questions are still unanswered. If I'm using HTTPS, I can be reasonably sure that the only parties who can decipher the communication are:

- myself
- the web server

But who is the web server really?

How do we know who we're talking to?

Near the little lock, many modern browsers will show you the name of the site you are connecting to. The first thing is to make sure that this is who you think it is. If you are about to send confidential information to your local credit union via their web page (e.g. lespeoples.org), you should be sure that the name near the lock is the name of your credit union. If the machine you are connecting to is something different (e.g. bigbadbank.com), then all the cryptography in the world won't help you keep your information private, because you are sending it to the wrong folks!

But if the name does match, there could still be problems: some nasty group could be intercepting your communications, and claiming to be the group you actually want to talk to. This isn't veering into paranoia here: the global network is very flexible; it relies on wide-scale co-operation; and the malicious actors are often tireless and conscienceless machines, not individual humans.

So how does your browser know to show that lock, since anyone could claim to be anyone else?

Browser lock showing tooltip

Because during the initial claim of identity, the web server presents a certificate which is cryptographically signed by an Certificate Authority (CA) who your browser already knows about and trusts. On some modern web browsers, if you hover your mouse over the lock, a tool tip will pop up showing which CA signed off on the certificate presented by the web server. In the image here, you can see that the authority who signed this certificate is Equifax.

Who do you trust?

But wait a minute! Who said that Equifax is an authority who can verify that folks are who they say they are? As any good anarchist would ask, why should you trust this authority? At the moment, you trust them implicitly because your web browser comes pre-configured to trust them. Many modern browsers ship with 30 or more of these CAs trusted automatically. If any one of these authorities is compromised or malicious, they could create fake certificates with whatever name they want. This means that, with only a few other small modifications, they could intercept (and tamper with) communications you intend to be private and untamperable.

Who are these authorities? Why are they included by default in our web browsers? Do they really do a good job in verifying identities before signing certificates? Do they have your best interests in mind? Do they share your political principles? If they received an unethical request from a corrupt governmental power or financial sponsor, would they comply, or would they resist?

I don't have the answers to these questions about any particular CA. But I think that the current technical infrastructure gives them incentives to behave in untrustworthy ways. We have very little reason to think that these CAs have the average web user (or server administrator) in mind when they decide policy, which makes our implicit trust in them all the more unjustified.

Relevant Architecture Components

What is it about the architecture of the Web that encourages this insecurity and lack of integrity? This requires a basic understanding of the underlying protocols used to create secure web connections. The Internet is a collection of co-operating machines, all passing messages to each other in various forms. Viewed from another angle, the Internet is also a collection of interacting protocols, which fit together in certain ways.

TLS

HTTPS is, at its root, HTTP (the common protocol by which web browsers talk to web servers) tunneled through Transport Layer Security, or TLS. TLS itself grew out of the Secure Sockets Layer, or SSL. TLS and SSL are generic protocols which define methods for encrypting any potentially lengthy bidirectional communications session. We call the side of the communications session that waits and listens for new connections the server, and the side that actively initiates connections the client. In the case of HTTPS, your web browser acts as a TLS client.

TLS (like many session-based protocols) begins with a handshake, which is used by the client and server to establish their shared assumptions. You can think of this as two complete strangers on a phone call: they run through the languages they speak, in an attempt to find a common language in which they can communicate.

Assuming both client and server find that each other speaks some common form of TLS, the handshake continues with the server offering the client a single certificate asserting the server's identity.

X.509 v3 certificates

The certificate presented is a combination of a cryptographic public key with an identifying name of the subject (typically the name of the server), where the combination of these two things is signed by a Certificate Authority. The signature is a statement by the Certificate Authority that the public key shown does in fact belong to the subject.

You can think of these three parts of the certificate as a state driver's license. The certificate's public key is sort of like the driver's license ID number. The certificate's subject is the driver's name, photo, and other identifying characteristics. The certificate's signature is like the hologram on a state driver's license. The DMV plays the role of the Certificate Authority. Only the DMV can make that hologram, and by applying it over the ID number and the statistics, the DMV is saying that this particular driver has this particular ID number. The specific format of the certificate used in TLS is not a driver's license, of course. It is specified by the X.509 standard.

X.509 covers a lot of different things, but for the purposes of this discussion, we're only interested in how it specifies the certificates used in TLS. In particular, I want to focus on two things: how the web server is identified, and how the signature is attached to the identity/public key combination.

The server is identified by a long string of which only the bit after the last CN= is really inspected by your web browser. Here's an example subject from a real-world certificate:

> /O=secure.mayfirst.org/OU=Domain Validated/OU=Go to https://www.thawte.com/repository/index.html/OU=Thawte SSL123 certificate/CN=secure.mayfirst.org

The identity of the signer (aka the issuer) is also present in the certificate, and a single signature is allowed within the certificate.

Your browser (or other TLS-capable client) takes the certificate, looks through its list of trusted certificate authorities for the signer. If it doesn't see the signer in that list, it treats the certificate as invalid. If the signer is present in the list of trusted CAs, your client uses information it already has about the signer to verify that the signature is in fact legitimate.

There's an extra step that can be thrown in here sometimes called certificate chaining, where the server presents not only its own certificate, but also the certificate of its issuer, where the assumption is that the issuer's own certificate is signed by a CA that the client already trusts.

But however the trust is followed, we end with one conclusion: the client must already know of and trust the ultimate signer of the certificate, and there can only be one ultimate signer for any certificate. If the client doesn't know of and trust that signer, they are merely guessing that the machine on the other end of the connection is the intended machine.

Concentration of Power, Financial Incentives, and Trust

So again, the question is: who are these Certificate Authorities? What is their background? Who operates them? What are their political convictions?

How does a typical certificate authority stay afloat?

The biggest Certificate Authority today at the beginning of 2007 is VeriSign. With their purchase of Thawte in 1999 and of GeoTrust in 2006, they are by far the largest issuer of certificates to the general public (over 70% in aggregate, according to Netcraft).

Verisign has a lot of other businesses, but it makes its CA money by selling certification to the entities requesting it. That is, if you decide to set up a new web site on a server named example.com, and you want to provide secured web access via https://example.com/, you might begin by paying VeriSign for a certificate that identifies your server as example.com. Why should VeriSign certify you with this name? For one thing, because you're paying them to do so. But their responsibility as a CA should include more rigorous checking. And they do so - but just a little bit more - often relying on the example.com DNS and email (both forgeable systems) to be configured properly and securely.

At any rate, the site operator is the one who foots the bill for the certificate, and the CA has little disincentive to turn down certification, since it would presumably mean they'd lose paying customers. If the CA were to engage in massive, wide-scale illegitimate certification, there's a possibility that browser vendors would drop them as a trusted root CA, but it would probably take a really large scandal, and it would likely take months (at least) for browser vendors to actively drop trust for the CA. This has never been done, as far as I know.

Who can be a Certificate Authority?

The kicker in all of this is that Verisign and the other commercial Certificate Authorities aren't using any expensive hardware or software to issue certificates. Free tools like OpenSSL or GnuTLS form the technical basis of most CAs, and there are free graphical frontends (like TinyCA) which make running a Certificate Authority a relatively simple task. These tools can be run on bottom-of-the-barrel hardware, and being a CA doesn't even require a heavy-duty connection to the Internet.

So if anyone can technically be a CA, how come people aren't doing it? For one thing, doing legitimate verification of identities is actually significant work. But the verification done by most CAs (including VeriSign) doesn't come close to this level of work, so that shouldn't be holding people back. It turns out the architecture of TLS itself discourages diversity.

Why does the architecture encourage concentration?

Remember that a TLS (HTTPS) server can only offer a single certificate. For hassle-free, secure connections, the signer of that certificate must already be trusted by the client (web browser). As a site administrator, you need to decide who is going to sign your certificate. Most browsers out there already trust the big corporate CAs. If a new independent CA were to spring up, it won't be trusted by any of the browsers, which means connections using a certificate from the new CA would likely cause errors for your site's visitors. Since you can only choose one, you probably will go with the existing Goliath, even if you feel no political affinity with them, and even if you resent paying money for their signature which could have been better used elsewhere.

As an individual who uses the web, your browser already trusts the big corporate CAs. Most of the web sites you visit are probably run by administrators who have made the trade off above. Why should you ask your browser to trust a new CA, even if it's one you personally actually trust more? It can be a hassle to maintain a list of trusted authorities, and it seems especially fruitless when the new authority you've added isn't actually used by any site that you visit. So why bother? And you're certainly not going to tell your browser to stop trusting the big corporate CAs, because nearly every site you visit has certificates issued by one of them.

What's worse, to make any change in the situation at all, there would need to be a massive break. The day that a site offers a new certificate signed by a new authority, every one of its visitors will see that cert, and will get errors if they don't already trust the new authority. The site administrator is pretty much guaranteed to cause problems for hir visitors by switching away from the mega-CAs.

This seems like a no-win situation, but there are ways out.

Alternate Architectures

The TLS architecture is the cause of this concentration of power, and changes to the architecture can permit or even encourage its dissolution.

What could change the incentives?

As usual, we need to follow the money. One of the reasons the big CAs have little reason to provide real security via heavy-duty verification before certification is because they lack significant competition. Making it easier to start and run a separate Certificate Authority, while actually encouraging its adoption would be a good thing.

If we were to modify the TLS protocol so that a server could offer multiple certificates at once, that would make it much easier to do a smooth transition away from un-trustworthy big CAs, because sites and users would no longer need the massive, disruptive transition that switching certificates would entail. One year, a web site could offer certificates from Verisign and a new, politically-active CA, while explaining to their users the reason for switching away, and then the next year, the site could drop the VeriSign certificate entirely.

An analogous change would be to enable multiple signatures on a single certificate. Recall that a single X.509 certificate contains a public key, a subject, and a signature binding the two together from a CA. There's no reason (in principle) that we couldn't declare a certificate as a public key, a subject, and a set of signatures, each from a different CA. It turns out that there is a proposal for this kind of alternate, multi-signature certificate (using the OpenPGP standard), which I'll talk about later.

But why should you trust a lot of small CAs more than a handful of big ones? The answer is that you wouldn't (and shouldn't) trust all the small CAs. You might trust a handful of smaller CAs, who you have a personal relationship with. Or you could spread your trust out over a wider range, deciding that you don't give full trust to any single CA. Instead, you could require certification by any 3 of the 20 CAs that you trust marginally. Although CA might be compromised, but it would be a harder job to infiltrate 3 of them.

If CAs are able to really compete on trustworthiness (which they can't right now because of the architecture), you could simply dismiss the CAs who are known to do a terrible job of verification, or who you don't trust for other reasons. For example why should you trust the Certificate Authority run by an oppressive government?

Once it becomes easier to phase in trust of new, alternative Certificate Authorities, we need to think about which ones technologically-aware activists would want to support. I suggest that a full change in the funding model is needed. Instead of being paid for by the site owner, a new-model Certificate Authority could operate independently, funded by its members who, by joining, help shape policy about what sort of verification should be required to grant a certificate.

With the ability to have multiple signatures, there's nothing stopping individuals from acting as their own CAs as well. Do you run your own web site? Certify it! Does your organization have a web site? You and your colleagues could each certify it. This sort of decentralization is healthy, fosters community networks, and can cut out the big corporate middlemen.

What else exists?

EV Certificates

The big corporate middlemen don't want to be cut out, of course. A plan is afoot from some of the larger CAs called Extended Validation (EV) Certificates. From what I can tell, this is simply the big CAs offering to actually do a serious level of identity verification - what they should have been doing all along! The bills for an EV cert, likely even heftier than usual, will probably continue to be paid by the sites requesting the certificates.

This does nothing to change the financial dynamics that make the system currently so untrustworthy. But it does relegate sites who can't pay the new larger fees to a second-class level of security, and it minimizes the number of entities considered officially capable of being an EV-cert-granting CA, further consolidating the power of the few at the top.

CACert.org

Another interesting player is CACert. This is a group that has set up to operate in the fashion of a typical certificate authority, but has set up a sophisticated, clear system explaining what it will take for them to grant you certification, based strictly on a network of trust built among their membership. This is a pretty good model, but it's a shame that they're the only one implementing anything like it. There should be multiple organizations with comparable models to this, so that each user could make hir own decisions about who they actually trust.

Another downside to CACert is the fact that their certificates are still issued only by one agency - the CACert CA. Even though they explicitly say they will only grant certificates according to their model, if their infrastructure is somehow compromised, it's possible for an attacker (or malicious employee) to issue certificates as CACert without following their published protocol.

Don't throw out the baby with the bathwater

All of this might seem more complicated than it needs to be; it's worth asking whether we need any of this at all. I want to make it clear that we do need secure communications. As activists, politically-outspoken workers, anti-authoritarians, or simply people who want to preserve our right to dissent, we need to be able to communicate to each other without eavesdropping or - worse - interference or impersonation. As members of a capitalist society, we are also purchasers and vendors of goods and services, and monetary donors and recipients. We need those transactions to be handled safely, so that we don't have our financial backing usurped.

More than just needing secure communications, we need secure communications without faceless, unaccountable, politically-fickle, mercenary gatekeepers. We need to take control of our own communications by taking responsibility for them.

Moving forward

So where can we go from here on the specific problem of the stunted TLS architecture?

An alternate architecture exists!

I mentioned earlier that there is an alternate proposal - OpenPGP Certificates instead of X.509 certificates - which allows multiple signatures per certificate. The proposal is designed to be implementable in parallel with existing X.509 certificates. However, it is not widely implemented or adopted yet.

Most programs which use TLS do not actually implement their TLS functionality directly. Instead, they make use of software libraries, which are collections of code that can be used by many programs.

At least one TLS library exists which can use OpenPGP certificates: the free GnuTLS library has supported OpenPGP certificates in addition to X.509 certificates since at least the end of 2003. Tools (like web browsers) which use the GnuTLS library basically can get this extra feature without any extra work.

However, the OpenSSL library is by far the most widely-used free library, and it only includes support for X.509 certificates. Some developers are discussing adding OpenPGP support for OpenSSL, but it's doubtful that anything will be ready in the near future. Tools which use OpenSSL are going to take a while to migrate to this new architecture.

So what needs to happen? Web browsers (and other TLS-enabled clients) need to start working with the new architecture. Web servers (and other TLS-enabled servers) need to start working with it as well.

One of the reasons to focus on Free Software (as covered by Amanda Hickman elsewhere in this book) is that we have an opportunity to contribute changes that we want to see. The big proprietary software makers may not share our agendas, or may actually be antagonistic.

Web Browser Buy-in

Mozilla Firefox is probably the widest-distributed Free Browser today. In my version of it on my Debian operating system, it actually already uses the GnuTLS library, but I haven't reviewed the sources to see how it gets used (it could be used for library features unrelated to certificate verification). Furthermore, there is no clear way through the Firefox graphical interface to manage OpenPGP CAs, the way there is to manage X.509 CAs. So that needs work. Firefox is also the basis for the proprietary Netscape browser, so any fix to Firefox could have an effect there. Many other Free browsers also derive from Firefox, so a fix here would be a big win.

Konqueror is another leading Free browser with an effect on other tools (Macintosh's Safari is based on Konqueror). It seems to use an SSL wrapper library (kssl) to talk to other libraries, but it appears to use OpenSSL exclusively at the moment. A fix to kssl to allow it to talk to GnuTLS would actually enable OpenPGP certificates for all the software in the KDE suite.

Finally, a couple of text-mode browsers, elinks and the venerable lynx appear to use the GnuTLS library these days.

Web Server Buy-in

Apache is the flagship Free web server. While the standard way to make apache work with TLS is the OpenSSL libraries via mod_ssl, a new module called mod_gnutls aims to make apache work with GnuTLS. However, mod_gnutls is still in its infancy, and is not clear if it is able to support OpenPGP keys or not.

Other web servers operate behind separate processes which handle all the TLS wrapping. These servers should be more easily switched to a library which supports OpenPGP. And gnutls-serv appears to offer itself as a rudimentary web server as well, if you needed a server to test browsers.

Next Steps

What can you do, yourself? Depending on how you use computers, there are different things you might want to do. If some of them seem confusing or you aren't sure how to start them, ask for help! There are web forums, mailing lists, and user groups filled with people who are interested in helping out.

All users

If you are a typical computer user these days, using standard tools, you can't switch to this new architecture all by yourself yet. But you can prepare yourself for a move to a more open, secure architecture in a number of ways:

- Adopt free software, which are the most likely tools to move to this new architecture first. Start with your web browser: If you are not using Mozilla Firefox, Konqueror, or some other free browser as your primary web browser, try to make the switch.
- Learn about encryption by setting yourself up with some tools. You can actually run GPG (an implementation of the OpenPGP standard) freely on any modern operating system. There are graphical front-ends and tutorials available online which might help you get a feel for managing certificates, signatures, and alternate authorities.

When using your web browser with normal HTTPS connections, start checking who the issuer is, and thinking about the chains of trust explicitly.

Webmasters

If you manage a website, and your site doesn't use HTTPS, consider offering it as an option so that your users can communicate with your site securely. For technical reasons, this will usually mean that you need your web site to have its own IP address. In the process of doing this, you'll also need to generate an X.509 certificate, as discussed here. You can either generate your own certificate (self-signed), get a commercial Certificate Authority to sign one for you, or you could ask for a cert from an alternate CA (such as CACert.org). Ask your system administrator if your web server is one of the few which supports OpenPGP certificates. If it does, generate and install one. If you're not sure how to do any of these steps, ask for help!

System Administrators

If you maintain a web server which offers HTTPS, consider offering support for OpenPGP certificates. If you administer an apache server, you might want to experiment with mod_gnutls where you would normally use mod_ssl.

Programmers

If you can read or write code, consider digging into one of the software packages above. If you see features that make sense but are not-yet ready for the public, test them and give feedback. If you see features that are needed but lacking, write up a proposal and pass it by the primary maintainer of the software, offering to implement it yourself if you think you can.

Who will be the new authorities?

If we do shift to this new architecture, who will offer these new-style certificates? Initially, I imagine that VeriSign and any other very big commercial CAs won't do it, because of the threat to their business model. But smaller CAs might be convinced to offer this service as an add-on to their existing business. And now groups like May First/People Link can simply and easily sign on as additional certifying agencies.

CACert.org already offers OpenPGP signatures, so it could probably be used immediately as an initial authority.

And most importantly, everyone who is aware and interested in these things can perform their own certifications, and publish them freely.

Back to the larger issue

This article goes into some technical detail on one particular corner of technical infrastructure that we use regularly, and looks at ways that architectural choices shape the social forces and structures attached to the infrastructure. But this is just one small corner. Most technological protocols we adhere to have social ramifications which are worthy of consideration. The Domain Name System, or DNS is another example: the US government at the moment wields a heavy influence over its direction because of some architectural choices, and the placement of a few key servers. This has international ramifications, and has actually caused some political tension recently.

The technical decisions made in the early days of email (as discussed in one of Jamie McClelland's articles in this book) continue to shape our lives and our communication choices today, and new extensions to the basic email protocols will continue to have impacts on how we can talk to each other.

Technical choices about how we store the music and movies that we make and listen to, documents and other data, all have social ramifications and are worthy of inspection and political consideration. And if the consideration reveals that there is technical work to be done to improve the social consequences, we need to take that work on, and support others who have similar social goals by adopting their work, even if it means occasional short-term inconvenience or cost.

If we make these social decisions in solidarity with each other, together we can build towards an egalitarian, democratic, non-hierarchical culture that spans the globe. The alternative is a fragmented society, where we are connected only to each other by the mechanisms of financial and cultural control, subjected to the whims of a small, powerful elite. So let's get to work!

The Email Crisis

by Jamie McClelland

For activists, possibly the most useful feature of the Internet is broken beyond repair.

If you use the Internet, you are certainly familiar with it. It's the tool that allows you to communicate with tens of thousands of people instantly. It allows activists from different countries, for the first time in history, to communicate and plan together at affordable costs. It's one of the few tools we have that breaks down artificial geographic barriers, enabling organizing on a scale never before imagined.

Email is broken.

This statement should come as no surprise to most users of email: deleting unwanted ads for Viagra and penis enlargers has become a routine daily exercise. Also - no surprise to any organizer who relies on mail delivery - the constant stream of bounces from providers like AOL or Yahoo who automatically reject our messages simply because they are being sent in bulk.

However, somehow, the Left does not seem to realize that this problem is primarily a political problem, not a technical problem.

The Email Problem

Let's consider: if we only understand the email problem as a technical problem, we could simply accept how the problem is understood by the mainstream media and the major corporations who are developing new solutions.

Problems (traditional view)

- Users get too many unsolicited email messages that are ads for things they have no need or desire for.
- Email users tend to blame the company that provides them with email service if they receive too many unsolicited email messages.
- Legitimate marketers and advertisers are not able to get their messages out.

If these are the problems, then the technical solutions follow.

Solutions (traditional view)

- Block messages suspected of being unsolicited (such as messages that are sent to more than 100 people or with certain words in the subject or body of the message) in such a way that the user never sees them. Then - the user thinks that their email provider "doesn't get spam" and is therefore a good provider.
- Create a certified email system. Legitimate advertisers pay a fee per email message sent that will not get blocked.
- Prevent users from sending email to more than 20 people at a time. If they are a legitimate advertiser then they should have the budget to afford a more expensive Internet service.
- Pass legislation that requires people to "double opt-in" for mailings. In other words, they must first request to be subscribed, then receive an email that requires them to click on a confirmation link in order to confirm that they want to be subscribed.
- Pass legislation that requires all bulk email to include a telephone number and postal address of the person responsible for the email.

On the other hand, if we understand the problem itself to be a political problem, we may describe both the problems and solutions differently. In fact,we may have new problems with the "solutions" identified above.

Politically Understanding the Spam Problem

What is spam anyway

Most people have no trouble at all separating the messages in their inbox that are spam from ones that are not spam. It's a fairly simple and immediate process. This truth may lead you to the belief that spam is something easy to define.

A cursory reading of material about spam reveals two common definitions: "Unsolicited Bulk Email" or "Unsolicited Commercial Email." Both definitions sound authoritative, and, if you are asked at a cocktail party to define spam, quoting either one will make you sound smart.

However, most people don't use these definitions when identifying which messages in their inbox are spam. For most of us, we read the subject line and see if we recognize the from address. No questions about whether it was sent in bulk, or what "commercial" really means. And, maybe we did solicit this information last year or maybe we did subscribe to that email list, but right now we don't want it. Therefore, it's spam.

Ultimately, despite volumes of web sites and Wikipedia to the contrary, the working definition of spam for most people is: "email that I don't want." There is a significant political difference between defining spam as "unsolicited bulk email" and "email that I don't want." The difference: who has the power to decide.

When spam is "objectively" defined, the email providers can "objectively" decide whether or not a message sent to you is spam - based on content filters identifying words commonly associated with commercial email, or indicators that more than one copy of the same message is being sent to their server. And, based on this objective determination, they can refuse delivery or outright delete the message before it ever reaches you.

This definition of spam is politically convenient for the email provider: once you accept it, it follows that the email provider can decide not to deliver certain email to a user. This definition ensures that providers need not offer a guarantee that they will deliver all of your email. On the other hand, defining spam as email that you don't want creates a very different set of expectations. If nobody but you can know if a certain email message is spam, then email providers must deliver all email and email users must have the tools to properly sort and filter what email they want to receive in their inbox.

The US has a curious perspective on the concept of censorship - namely, it is only a problem if it is perpetuated by the government. Imagine the political outrage if the US postal service decided to trash 2000 postcards sent to a particular town by a peace group. There would be no question that the rights of the residents of that town and the rights of the peace group were violated. However, when Yahoo does precisely that with political email, it is considered an understandable strategy to fight spam.

The effect of shifting our political understanding of spam is more freedom and rights for email users, coupled with more responsibility. Yes, it is more work to take responsibility for sorting and filtering our own email, and yes, there is a learning curve, and yes, as a movement, it is politically imperative that we learn how to do these things for ourselves.

Certified email

AOL drew a brief amount of criticism in early 2006 when it announced it's partnership with Goodmail. Goodmail is one of many corporations that provide email "certification." Anyone who wants to send bulk email can apply to Goodmail. Goodmail, somehow, determines whether they are a "legitimate" bulk email sender. Then, the bulk email sender encodes an encrypted key into each email message they send. When AOL receives this email, their systems verify the key. Since AOL has decided to trust Goodmail, they allow any message with this key to pass through all spam filters and end up in the user's inbox.

The part of the announcement that drew the firestorm was that AOL would *only* be using Goodmail to determine if an email message should be able to by-pass their spam detection filters. Previously, AOL had used a free, public system where anyone could apply to AOL to bypass their spam filters.

AOL, with great agility, modified their proposal as minimally as possible to take all the steam out of the campaign opposing it. They announced they would keep their free white listing system (although that system would still be subjected to certain filters not subjected to Goodmail email). In addition, they announced that 501(c)(3) nonprofit organizations would be entitled to apply for another email certification process that would be free. They maintained the Goodmail option, which still is available as of the writing of this essay.

So, what's the problem?

Perhaps the most revolutionary aspect of the Internet is the inherent direct democracy ingrained into the very protocols that govern it's operation. If you connect your computer to the Internet, you are part of the Internet, and an equal part at that. You can send email to as many people as you want, you can drive as many people as you can to view your web site. There's no need to build an expensive television studio or a power radio transmitter.

The very concept of a single-authority, corporate-run, certified email system runs counter to this democratic ideal. The acceptance of certified email, even as one of many options employed by AOL or any other major email provider, threatens our ability as organizers to use the Internet, period. It threatens to make the Internet another medium that, like the broadcasting medium, requires a substantial capital investment to use. Certified email is a real threat to the left.

Remarkably, this development has passed under the radar of the left. With the exception of the Dear AOL campaign (which was composed mostly of technologists), the rest of the left has remained on the sidelines.

Double Opt-In

The solution offered by many critics of certified email and other restrictive practices designed to stem the tide of spam is to enforce a rigorous set of privacy guidelines to determine when it is OK to send bulk email to an email address.

This idea of double opt-in often figures prominently among these guidelines. This concept means: you must ask twice to be put on a list.

For interactions that only happen on the Internet, this guideline is essential. If I enter my email address on a web site indicating that I want to subscribe to an email newsletter, a confirmation message should be sent to my email address, and I should be required to click on a link provided in that email message to confirm that I want to be subscribed. This step is required because anyone in the world can enter anyone else's email address on a web form.

However, too often the concept of double opt-in is taken too far.

If I'm organizing a community garden and ten people from my neighborhood come to the first meeting, and everyone gives me their email address because they want to participate in organizing the garden via email, according to the rules of "double opt-in" I should send them an email invitation to join the list and count on them to click the link that will enable them to participate. Never mind if some of them joined the Internet for the first time six months ago and are not fully aware of what it means to confirm a subscription to an email list. Never mind if some of them spent days working up the courage just to come to the meeting and, while wanting the community garden, are afraid that they don't fit in or belong. Never mind if some of them share their email address with someone else who is liable to delete the invitation. Never mind if some of them don't have a full command of English and are not likely to understand what the email invitation says.

If, historically, organizers had followed this principle during any political struggle in the world, the world would be a different place. If organizers had to ask permission before knocking on a door or making a phone call, then we'd have far fewer organizations. The world is not a friendly place for getting two or more people together to do something creative. The only way that happens is by spending every ounce of our energy and resources creating the opportunity for people to cooperate - not by creating barriers for this cooperation.

While this line of thinking may sound obvious to organizers, it is not always obvious to progressive technologists, and that means organizers need to be more involved in shaping the development of the Internet.

Identity

There is no commonly used method for determining that the person sending email really is the person they say they are.

It is a common misconception about email that the "From:" address has any meaning or validity at all. For the record: it does not. Anybody can send email to anybody else and put any arbitrary email address in the from line. For example, if you use Thunderbird as your email client, try playing around with the "Identities" feature - it allows you to define any arbitrary from address that you like. This can be fun: send email to your friends from `che.guevara@revolution.org`! Of course, this issue is not a Thunderbird security issue - it is a security issue that is fundamental to email itself.

This issue is related to spam - most spammers forge their "From:" address, which is why filtering email based on the "From:" address (either to filter out addresses that send spam or to filter in messages from your friends) is not a good strategy. However, it is a much bigger issue for activists, particularly those of us building political coalitions that go through periods in which one poorly written (or forged) email message can cause firestorms that are difficult to over come.

Even more sensitive: consider the way most email lists operate, particularly announcement-only email lists. These tools are commonly setup to only allow messages to be posted from a certain approved email address. That is correct: the only thing preventing most email lists from sending unauthorized email messages is a little twiddling about in our Thunderbird "Identities" configuration.

This is bad.

There are solutions that are available and highly effective on an individual basis. Most notably is Open Pretty Good Privacy (OpenPGP), an Internet standard for signing and encrypting email messages. Using OpenPGP, you can digitally "sign" your email message in such a way that recipients of your email know that it was sent by you.

However, this technology is difficult to conceptually understand (particularly the important "web of trust" aspects) and, more importantly, the movement has not made this technology a political priority. To date, May First/People Link has never, in our long history of providing technical support to the left, received a request to help setup OpenPGP.

Future thinking

Even if we were to start using OpenPGP effectively, even if we were able to re-define spam as "Email I don't want," even if we were to re-write the rules about how bulk email should be sent, we would have a functional system for exchanging messages (which is good) in which anywhere from 50 - 90% of our resources was spent exchanging email that is not wanted (which is bad).

The Email Crisis

Over the last year alone, the amount of computer resources and labor that May First/People Link has devoted to email has risen dramatically and at a precariously non-sustainable rate.

If we want to build infrastructure, owned and run by the movement, to deliver our email, we will eventually need a more efficient system. Whereas highly capitalized corporations will continue throwing money and faster computers at the problem, enabling them to continue delivering email even when the volume of unwanted messages continues to grow, our movement will not be able to keep up.

As a movement, we are dependent on email. Email has become so intertwined into our daily organizing routine that if it becomes unworkable, it would take years for us to fully adjust to a new system.

For that reason, it is critical that we begin to consider alternatives now.

And, the alternatives must be firmly rooted in our politics.

FOSS and Proprietary Software

Software Freedom

by Amanda B. Hickman

Mary Harris Jones never kept a blog. Not one person got an email urging them to Selma in 1965. César Chávez didn't have a database of United Farm Workers membership. Ten years ago, we were organizing without computers; today, an organizer without email is almost unthinkable. As activists and organizers we depend upon tools that are owned and patented by people whose fundamental perspective on how the world's resources should be used and shared, of how the world should look, directly contradicts our own. If you are working towards a just and ecologically sustainable world, you're with me in this contradiction. This isn't simply a philosophical conundrum: it could have real, practical ramifications on our work and ability to organize.

YouTube is very cool, and potentially a great tool, but I recently watched as a media activist grabbed the mouse to show us the clip he'd recently posted on YouTube and the intensive discussion surrounding it. I don't recall now what the video was about, because I never saw it – what we all saw instead as the page loaded was a notice: "This video may contain content that is inappropriate for some users, as flagged by YouTube's user community." We'd have to create an account to view the clip. A minor hurdle, but how many more people would have seen their content without that hurdle?

If no one objects to what you have to say, then you've got nothing to worry about. But as organizers, if we are putting technology and technological infrastructure at the core of our organizing strategies, it matters that we own the infrastructure we use. This is not a new concern, although as we rely ever more on networked technology, the risks are more pronounced. The same networks that evolved from a military need for decentralized communications now allow all kinds of centralized access to information about what software we are running on our laptops and workstations. Patents may protect printing press technologies or radio micro transmitters, but unlawful use of borrowed software licenses and patented technology is far easier to detect and intervene to prevent than illegal replication of a patented radio transmitter will ever be.

Today, the same media conglomerates now smarting at the persistent affront of public radio and cable access are looking at the Internet and thinking hard about how to avoid sharing any of it. Proprietary software is one mechanism that media conglomerates would like to use to lock in their control over the Internet.

What is Free and Open Source Software?

Though you could go your whole computer using life without reading a single software license through, you agree to one just about every time you install software on your computer. The license - your license to use the software - lays out what you can do with the software you are about to install and who is responsible when something goes wrong (usually, not the manufacturer). Licenses can break out your rights in a variety of ways, but fundamentally, the license dictates whether or not you can share the software with other users (and under what circumstances), what you can use the software for, and who can make changes to the software.

Free and Open Source Software (FOSS, for short) can be freely redistributed, analyzed and modified by anyone. The "source" or "source code" is the stuff that the programmers write: instructions to the computer that make the program go. Free and open source software is always:

- Free: You are free to use and modify the software for any purpose. Your license to use or modify the software is limited only by the requirement that you not limit others' freedom to do likewise.
- Open: Source code distributed with the software can be modified by anyone with programming skills (and re-released as a usable application). Unlike proprietary software where the code that runs a program is hidden, anyone can view the code that runs a FOSS application and make their own modifications to it.
- Collaborative: Programmers who improve, modify or customize programs and then re-distribute them must make their changes, improvements and modifications available in the same free and open manner.

Consider the difference between buying a car that is delivered with the hood welded shut and a car that comes with an annotated diagram of the engine and a hood that opens with a standard tool. Consider the automotive tinkerer who decides to open that welded engine and make it more fuel efficient: she can benefit from that tinkering herself, but if she tries to share her knowledge with anyone but the manufacturer, she's breaking the law. By contrast, a free and open source car explicitly allows her to make it more efficient, with the proviso that should she decide to sell her souped up engine, she can't weld the bonnet shut herself. Moreover, she has her choice of competent (and incompetent!) mechanics when she needs professional intervention.

Programmers who contribute to the development of a free and open source application know that no one can take away their right to benefit from the labor they have devoted to a project. As a result, Free Software benefits from the input, scrutiny and innovation of many users and developers.

How does software become free? The people who created it release it under a license such as the General Public License (GPL) that meets the criteria outlined above. One of the terms of this license is that programmers who modify a piece of software and re-distribute it must release their own modifications under the same open, free and collaborative conditions of the original software.

Software licenses, even open source ones, vary widely, and many otherwise free and open licenses don't require that derivative works be shared freely. There are many different licenses that meet the criteria of the "free software definition" and so can be used to release free and open source software. If you are intrigued by the finer points of software freedom, or the subtle political distinctions between "free software" and "open source software" there is a lot of good writing out there, both at the Open Source Institute and at the Free Software Foundation.

Why should I use free and open source software?

It might surprise you that the first answer is not "because it doesn't cost anything." Software is never without cost: every technological tool or application requires some work on your part. Most users choose one application over another simply because someone they trust is already using it. Very often, people don't even "choose" software. We use what seems to be standard, and don't give the matter much thought. If it doesn't come with our computers, we buy (or borrow) the software we need to do our work, either from a manufacturer directly, a local consultant or the bootleg CD market. The price you pay for a software license is a fragment of what it costs to own that software and rely on it. Technical support, training, upgrades: these things cost time and money. Time you spend learning how to maximize your use of an application is an investment.

Most NGOs have most of the tools they need for day to day work, or they've stitched together a workable solution. When organizations do think about the cost of software, they think about whether they could pay less for what they need.

Often, free and open source software is less expensive. If, as an organization, you commit yourself to proprietary and potentially expensive software to meet your book keeping or layout (or word processing or membership management or graphics editing) needs, you will eventually face new expenses.

Moreover, though quality photo editing and layout software might be easy to steal now (and that is what you are doing when you buy a single user CD and install it on every computer in the office, or when you "borrow" an installation disk from someone else or buy a duplicated disk) most core applications are likely to become much harder to install without valid licenses in the near future. Programs like Microsoft Office and Adobe Photoshop have already dramatically improved their ability to detect duplicate installations on a network. If you want to share responsibility for a project that requires specialized software, you may find that you need software to run on multiple desktops. If you don't want to pay for multiple site licenses, you should take a look at free and open source applications.

The alternative to free and open source software is a cumbersome network of licenses and patents and laws that don't acknowledge the role that users play, over time, in testing, developing and fine tuning software applications, and whole economies dependent on a monoculture of tools. As a result, a software company holds the reins even though users worldwide have put enormous work into adapting to their tools, reporting bugs, requesting features, identifying innovations and workarounds.

If your own work is part of a movement, you can contribute to that movement by using free and open source software. When you use software, any software, you are collaborating with the programmers and developers who learn, from your work, how to make the tools they are building work better. By collaborating in the development of software tools that you need to do your work well, you are helping build infrastructure that makes that software better. When that software is Free and Open Source, it is accessible to other users, whether or not they can afford licenses or are eligible for license discounts.. Better, more accessible tools can make everyone's work stronger.

You don't have to grind to a halt and master a whole new set of tools today in order to start using free software. You could, however, look at some of the tools you rely on now and start looking for free software that will meet some of the same needs. Install OpenOffice.org (or NeoOffice, if you've got a Mac) and try getting to know it – when a new version of Microsoft Office comes out, you'll be in a much better position to decide whether it is worth the expense. MediaWiki, which you can run in a private directory on your web server, will allow you to edit documents collaboratively – this is the software behind Wikipedia. Try it out next time you need to collaborate with someone on a document. The GIMP (GNU Image Manipulation Program) is a great image editing application, and it is free software. OpenOffice, GIMP and MediaWiki are three of hundreds of FOSS tools that you could be using in your day-to-day work.

You have the opportunity to join an international network of people who are committed to using, creating and sharing free software tools. If you use free and open source software, you make free tools more widely available to other organizations like your own, both by reporting bugs and inconsistencies and by showing that it can be done.

What is an Operating System?

A single computer is nothing more than a circuit board, some microchips and a big storage disk (or not so big, depending on your computer). A microchip on the circuit board stores a simple program that handles basic functioning: a clock and a process for starting up. To do anything useful with the machine, you need an operating system - software that runs on your hard disk and facilitates fancy things like displaying a graphical interface on your screen and managing the memory needs of the different software widgets and applications that you use to work.

As it happens, there are dozens of computer operating systems to choose from, most of which you'll never hear about. Three that are in common use include Mac OSX and Microsoft Windows both proprietary operating systems; and GNU/Linux, a free and open source operating system. Builds of GNU/Linux exist to run on almost any model of microprocessor in production.

Almost everything you do with your computer, short of precariously balancing bowls of soup atop it, relies on the operating system. You can run a great many free software applications on a proprietary operating system like the Mac OS or MS Windows. Or, you can run a free and open source operating system.

Even if you choose to run a Free and Open Source operating system on your computer, there are proprietary applications available - Adobe Acrobat Reader, Flash players, Skype - that you can install and run on an otherwise free software system. If you're used to working in Microsoft Windows or Mac OSX, switching over to a GNU/Linux computer probably won't be painless, but it can be done. GNU/Linux is available in dozens of "distributions." They each vary slightly, but any distribution with an active user community will do. Ubuntu Linux, in particular, has an active base of desktop users - regular people running Ubuntu on the computer they use every day. You can try Ubuntu (or another Linux distribution) on the computer you use now by booting from a live CD. Most computers will, by default, try to boot from the CD, rather than the hard drive, when a CD is present. When you boot from a live CD, the operating system and software loads from the disk. You can run Linux until you eject the CD and reboot. Your old operating system will still be there, unchanged. Making the switch to a new operating system is a bit easier if you're starting from scratch with a new computer, but if you have access to a spare computer, you could install Linux on it. At the very least, next time you are contemplating an expensive upgrade to your operating system, consider that it might be a good time to move to a Free and Open Source operating system.

If you want to use Free Software, you have a fundamental choice to make: do you want to use a free and open source operating system or will you run free software on a proprietary operating system?

Isn't this stuff patented?

Software manufacturers, feeling the pinch, seek out patent and copyright protection from Free Software competition, but software isn't the only arena in which corporations have sought and continue to seek patents that shield them from any competition at all. Some intellectual property radicals will argue that no knowledge should be owned by a single entity, because invariably their ability to patent information is only evidence that they got the patent application in first. It isn't an easy question, but it is one worth asking: should anyone be able to "own" an idea?

The patent system was designed to promote "the progress of science and the useful arts" by securing inventors right to use their inventions. When corporations use patent law to prevent anyone else from providing a service that the world was looking for long before that patented innovation came along, they're abusing the protection that patents are designed to provide. When a pesticide manufacturer can add some twist, a hybridization or genetic modification, to a seed variety that is already the product of hundreds of years of agricultural stewardship, experimentation with crop hybridization and seed saving by indigenous (and not-so-indigenous) farmers, and patent that modification, they're effectively capping off centuries of knowledge and innovation. Until Monsanto began using patent law to protect seed hybrids, each successive hybrid or farming technique could be shared, passed on. Farmers and agricultural scientists could learn from one another, share knowledge and, together, develop a valuable body of information. No one can build on Monsanto's innovations without explicit permission from Monsanto: that has a dramatic impact on the future and progress of agricultural knowledge. Variations on this pattern are widely repeated in medicine, where pharmaceutical companies have been allowed to patent not just the precise cure they've developed, but the idea of a cure for the disease in question at all.

On the Internet, abuses of contemporary patent law are equally pronounced, though they don't threaten global food security quite as dramatically. Patent resellers, who make a business of licensing patents without ever offering any service or product themselves, hold patents to an impressive array of dynamic website features. Amazon.com technically holds a patent on the one click checkout process, and any online vendor who organizes their site such that shoppers can buy an item in a single mouse click is infringing on that patent. In fact, almost every conceivable element of a web-based retailer is protected by one patent or another, from previews of product images to accepting rebate codes.

In many cases, the Public Patent Foundation[1] has taken up the task of contesting overly broad patents or patents on knowledge that belongs in the public realm, but patent law in the US and abroad could very well stand in the way of organizers' ability to get and use the tools that they need to work.

Myths about Free and Open Source Software

Start asking around about free and open source software and you'll hear some grand promises along with some damning critiques. Here are some common myths about FOSS:

Myth: Free and Open Source Software is virus-proof.

Truth: there are far fewer viruses that attack open source software applications, in part because fewer people use FOSS. The simple fact that an application is free and open source does not mean it will be any more or less susceptible to viruses or spyware: that depends on how well the application is written and how many developers are actively monitoring that software. Nonetheless, you will have fewer problems with viruses and spyware if you stop using (in roughly this order) Internet Explorer, Outlook, Microsoft Office, Microsoft Windows.

Myth: Free and Open Source Software doesn't work

Truth: Some free software works, some doesn't. Same as proprietary software. There are programmers who have put years of energy and expense into proprietary website content management systems that have

1 http://www.pubpat.org/

never worked well and will never work well and cost enormous amounts of money. The quality of free and open source software applications varies as widely as that of proprietary software.

Myth: FOSS is made by volunteers, so you shouldn't expect too much of it

Truth: This is one of the most persistent misunderstandings about Free and Open Source Software. Without a doubt, some FOSS applications are built by volunteers, acting entirely out of altruism. More often than not, however, FOSS developers are compensated for their work, and expected to meet some standards of quality. Sometimes a developer is customizing or extending an existing application to meet the specifications of a paying client; often developers who are hired to do custom work will insist on a contract that clearly states that their work will be released as FOSS, as an alternative to a work for hire agreement under which the client owns the product of their labor and the developer doesn't even retain the right to reuse the application in their own work.

People providing technical support on lists and forums often aren't being paid for their time, and are helping you out because someone helped them out once and they are passing on the favor. If you find that free support resources are inadequate, you may need to look into paid support options.

Myth: Open Source Software is not secure

Truth: Security is an important consideration when choosing software. Established and long standing open source applications are often more secure than their proprietary counterparts. This sometimes surprises folks who assumed that openness makes software less secure, but being able to review source code doesn't mean that a programmer can disrupt a working installation. It means that anyone with the skills to identify a structural flaw can point it out, and propose a solution. Proprietary software relies on the obscurity of its workings, but dedicated hackers will find holes in anything, and they do. Windows is highly vulnerable to viruses and other malware: obscurity of its code hasn't spared it.

Myth: Big and powerful organizations use expensive proprietary software

Truth: Some organizations with deep pockets do use expensive proprietary software, but many influential organizations such as Greenpeace or the ACLU, are using Free software to manage massive websites or donor databases. If you know someone who works for a large union or other organization, ask them what they use and then ask whether it works for them. Often you'll find that actually thousands of member records are trapped in an expensive and proprietary fundraising database that doesn't meet their needs. They continue to use it because the cost of migration is prohibitive.

Myth: All free software is Free

Truth: Some people like to use Latin-based "gratis" and "libre" to distinguish between software that is free of charge (gratis), like Acrobat Reader, Skype, AIM or free beer; and software that is free (libre) to be modified, shared, improved and used by you and anyone else. When we talk about Free software in this essay, we're talking about software that is Free, as in freedom. Often, it is also gratis.

Conclusion

You have a choice about the software you use and the community you build around it, and each software decision you make should be made with that in mind: you do have a choice, and very often, free and open source tools are available that will meet your needs and allow you to help make sure that other organizers will also have access to the tools they need to do their work. For more ideas about free and open source tools that activists and organizers are using, take a look at: the NGO in a Box project[1], the Nonprofit Open Source Initiative[2] and the Social Source Commons[3]. To learn more about software freedom and the role of patents in information and communications technology, take a look at the Free Software Foundation[4], the Electronic Frontier Foundation[5] and the Public Patent Foundation[6].

Portions of this document were adapted from these valuable publications on using Open Source Software in Non-Profit organizations:

Choosing and Using Open Source Software: A Primer for Non- Profits, (2003, Nonprofit Open Source Initiative) by Michelle Murrain with Rich Cowan, Reuben Silvers, Anders Schneiderman, Amanda Hickman and Jamie McClelland

Choosing Open Source: A guide for civil society organizations (2004, Association for Progressive Communications) by Mark Surman and Jason Diceman.

1 http://www.ngoinabox.org/
2 http://www.nosi.net/
3 http://www.socialsourcecommons.org/
4 http://www.fsf.org/
5 http://www.eff.org/
6 http://www.pubpat.org/

About the Authors

Alfredo López is co-director of May First/People Link. He has been involved in movements for social change for 40 years as an organizer and coordinator of several mass demonstrations and events as well as a leader in the Puerto Rican Independence movement. He's the author of six books and many articles and has produced several video documentaries and a two-season television news series.

Amanda B. Hickman is the Director of Technology at GothamGazette.com and is on the steering committee of the Nonprofit Open Source Initiative (NOSI). She was recently the Senior Circuit Rider at the LINC Project of the Welfare Law Center where she provided technology assistance and training to low-income grassroots groups in the US working on anti-poverty issues. Previously she taught "Digital Activism"; an undergraduate course on using the internet as an organizing tool at NYU's Gallatin School. She is also an active local organizer who (always in collaboration with others) founded Greene Acres Community Garden and runs a public compost drop-off at the Fort Greene Farmer's Market.

Daniel Kahn Gillmor is a technology advisor who works with nonprofit, educational, and activist groups in NYC. He is a firm believer that people should be in control of their information and the tools they use instead of the other way around, and tries to help these groups regain control. He has been breaking computers and fixing them again for over 20 years, and is currently involved in the Debian project, helping to improve a great Free operating system.

Jamie McClelland is a co-director of May First/People Link, a unionized, membership-based Internet hosting organization. In addition to the expected duties of system administration, support, and programming projects, he's actively involved in organizing technologists around the US Social Forum. In one capacity or another, Jamie has spent the last eight years providing technology support to nonprofits and activist organizations. Prior to technology work, Jamie has worked in a variety of organizations and movements, including Libraries for the Future, Act Up!, and ACORN.

Eric Goldhagen is a technology worker with a background in journalism and print production, and a history as a media/technology/social justice activist. He is a Partner at Openflows Community Technology Lab, Inc., a founding member of the InterActivist Network, and part of the Autonomedia publishing collective. He can be found in his off hours at the public access computer facility he started in 1998 at ABC No Rio, a community center on the Lower East Side of Manhattan.

A Word About May First/People Link

All the authors of this book are members of May First/People Link, an organization of progressive activists and organizations who use the Internet's technology in their work and are committed to the Internet's continued growth and freedom.

For more information about MF/PL, please visit its website:

http://www.mayfirst.org/

A Word about this Book

This book was created with free software. The text of the book was written and edited collaboratively using MediaWiki (http://www.mediawiki.org/), and the page layout was done with OpenOffice.org (http://www.openoffice.org/). The cover was built primarily in Inkscape (http://www.inkscape.org/). The font family used is DejaVu (http://dejavu.sourceforge.net/), a free and open source font. The 9 point type is smaller than that used in many commercially published books; that's to save on paper and expense.

The Future of this Book

This book, like the Internet itself, is the product of ongoing discussion and collaboration. After the book is published, we expect these ideas to continue growing and evolving, and we hope that our readers will join expand these discussions as well. You can find follow up details about the book, errata, and discussion online at:

http://www.mayfirst.org/organicinternet/

We hope you'll join us!